It must have been providential that I wa this book. It must have been provident. my inbox while I was stranded for days (home. It must have been providential that ....would most be tempted to grumble and complain about my circumstances, I had already set aside the time to read it. But certainly it was the right book at the right time. And I'm quite certain it will prove to be the same for you.

TIM CHALLIES
Author of *Seasons of Sorrow*

The Apostle Paul declares that contentment must be learned (Phil. 4:12), and David Kaywood's book has much to teach us about this rare jewel that is worth learning about. In our restless world we need to find rest in the One who alone can satisfy. I was encouraged by this book to do just that. I recommend it.

BILL KYNES
Retired pastor and Council member, The Gospel Coalition;
Senior Fellow for Pastoral Theology at the C.S. Lewis Institute

Most Christians see the way our culture has refashioned certain sins into virtues. We notice, for example, when old words like sexual immorality become seen as virtuous self-expression. But have we noticed the shift with discontentment? Rise and grind, we're told. Never be satisfied. Have at least one side hustle, maybe two. I'm thankful David Kaywood not only sounds the alarm in A Call to Contentment, but he also offers a way out of our frothy mess of anxiety into the calm of godly satisfaction.

BENJAMIN VRBICEK
Pastor, Community Evangelical Free Church; Harrisburg, Pennsylvania;
managing editor for Gospel-Centered Discipleship

We have so much, but we still struggle to feel content. The solution isn't more; it's to discover and apply what Scripture teaches. That's why I'm grateful for this book by David Kaywood. It's biblical, insightful, and practical. My copy is full of highlights to review and apply; I'm sure yours will be too. It's such a helpful book on a topic that really matters for God's glory and the good of our souls.

DARRYL DASH
Pastor, Grace Fellowship Church, Don Mills, Toronto;
author of *How to Grow* and *Eight Habits for Growth*

Convicting and practical! *A Call to Contentment* shines the light of Scripture on our generation's besetting sin, exposing the many ways we become ensnared by discontentment and helping readers to understand, apply, and cultivate that sweet and precious attitude of Christ-honoring contentment regardless of life circumstances.

REAGAN ROSE
Founder of Redeeming Productivity

A

call

to

CONTENTMENT

PURSUING GODLY SATISFACTION
IN A RESTLESS WORLD

A

call

to

CONTENTMENT

DAVID KAYWOOD

Copyright © David Kaywood 2024

paperback ISBN 978-1-5271-1099-1
ebook ISBN 978-1-5271-1143-1

10 9 8 7 6 5 4 3 2 1

Published in 2024
by
Christian Focus Publications Ltd,
Geanies House, Fearn, Ross-shire,
IV20 1TW, Great Britain.

www.christianfocus.com

Cover design by Pete Barnsley (CreativeHoot)

Printed and bound by
Bell & Bain, Glasgow

For Denise,

my loyal and faithful wife.

Contents

"Next to faith this is the highest art: to be content with the calling in which God has placed you."
— Martin Luther

"You say, 'If I had a little more, I should be very satisfied.' You make a mistake. If you are not content with what you have, you would not be satisfied if it were doubled."
— Charles Spurgeon

Part 1:

Understanding Contentment

Chapter 1
What is Contentment?

"The comprehensiveness of our contentment is another measure whereby we may judge whether we really know God." — J.I. Packer

con·tent·ment |\ ken-'tent-ment*noun*

1. the freedom from dependence on desired circumstances that comes from God's empowering grace to endure everything with rejoicing
2. that sweet, inward, quiet, gracious frame of spirit, which freely submits to and delights in God's wise and fatherly disposal in every condition[1]
3. An inward state of satisfaction independent of circumstances

***

I almost died when I was a baby. A sizeable hole in my heart led the doctors to wonder if I was going to survive. Many tears flowed from my mother's eyes as she eagerly waited until her middle child was old enough to have open-heart surgery. "You looked blue," she said, when as an adult I asked about my appearance. I was unusually skinny and malformed. When my grandmother first saw me as a baby, she told my mom I should get baptized immediately.

It took a few years of hospital visits for me to completely recover. Although my heart defect understandably frightened my mom, my slow start in life hasn't deterred me too much. Of course, there is the large scar down my chest. For some reason I was required to take penicillin before going to the dentist. And my breathing at times

---

1. Jeremiah Burroughs, *The Rare Jewel of Christian Contentment* (Carlisle: The Banner of Truth Trust, 1964), 19.

3

sounds raspy, which was painfully brought to my attention when a football teammate asked, "Why are you breathing like that?" during senior-led conditioning week for high school football training. "David always breathes like that," replied a senior varsity captain.

During my junior year in high school, our football team made it to the Varsity Football State Championship game where over 20,000+ screaming fans met at a stadium in St. Louis to watch a bunch of teenagers play with a ball. Making it to the state championship game was thrilling, but I was also crushed during that season of life because at the same time, my youngest brother was dying from heart failure. Our team was favored to win, but by halftime the game was nearly over. During his half-time speech, coach yelled at us and said we need to stop acting like babies because people like David's brother actually have a reason to be sad, but we don't.

Cardiomyopathy was the official diagnosis. His heart was abnormally large and had a difficult time pumping blood to his body. At fifteen, he got on the waiting list for a heart transplant. I remember helping him carry his book bag through the hallways in high school. I looked blue as a baby, but he looked pale. His eyelids were dark too. Confusion and despair struck our household as we wondered what would happen to the baby of the family. A heart organ match arrived just before it was too late for my brother. God often waits until the last second to act to teach us to trust him.

Athletic ability runs in my family. My other brother was a captain of a well-respected college football program that made several national championship appearances. There were high expectations for him going into his junior year, but his progress would be derailed. While sleeping during one January evening, he awoke to his apartment complex completely on fire. The small-town fire department eventually arrived, but the fires were getting closer to his apartment. The back and forth dialogue between my brother and the firefighters to determine how to orchestrate an escape ended when the smoke, now on him, forced him to jump out of his apartment window to save his life. Tragically, another tenant died.

His leap to save himself brought national attention, but the fire left a third of his body permanently scarred.

I was baptized the summer before I started college, after watching both of my brothers almost die. I was excited about grace but confused about life. Why did God send all of these family difficulties? Maybe you've had similar hardships and have asked, "Why have I experienced so many trials in my life?" I resonate with the Apostle Paul who uses the word "perplexed" when he speaks of his personal suffering: "We are afflicted in every way, but not crushed; perplexed, but not driven to despair" (2 Cor. 4:8). He trusted God, but by no means did he understand the reason behind all of his trials. But maybe he wasn't supposed to. God, after all, doesn't teach you contentment like magic; he teaches you contentment by placing you in situations that require you to learn contentment.

In an increasingly secular twenty-first century that wants the people of God to look to anything and everything besides the Christian faith for personal meaning, value, and purpose, Christian contentment must be learned in order to spiritually thrive. While the Christians who don't learn contentment won't look much different than the secular culture, the Christians who do learn contentment will not only spiritually flourish, but will also be a shining light in a hostile society. Learning contentment will lead others to ask about "the hope that is in you" (1 Pet. 3:15).

The Problem

Suppose your favorite figure from church history or your great-great grandparent or a deceased person from over a century ago were suddenly planted in a Western country today. What would they see? They would see grocery stores offering unlimited food options at affordable prices. They would be stunned at a microwave's power to cook food in minutes. Air-conditioning, heating, and cozy homes would no doubt amaze them. So too would electric lighting, widely accessible clean water, and indoor plumbing. They would be glad to know that backbreaking toil or the family business would not be the only available career path for them since there are now thousands of college and university options to foster education with the hopes of landing a satisfying career. It would be liberating for them to discover the invention of antibiotics, eliminating the horror of possibly one day getting polio, smallpox, or measles.

The person in your mind would encounter a smartphone or computer allowing them access to almost anything they ever wanted to know in seconds. They may decide to engage in one of the endless options for entertainment like television or a podcast. They could even take advantage of same-day travel or connect with someone in a different part of the world through the internet. The dramatic rise in life expectancy would probably surprise them, since it was not uncommon for people to die young back in their day. This figure in your head would look at the widespread prosperity and significant increase in comfort and quality of living and conclude that all of these unprecedented advancements in almost every area of life have made everyone in the world substantially happier.

But they would be wrong.

"Over the last five centuries, and especially over the last 100 years," says one writer, "many nations of the world have experienced an astounding increase in material prosperity that is unlike anything seen before in the history of the world."[2]

But has prosperity led to contentment?

In his book, *The Progress Paradox: How Life Gets Better While People Feel Worse*[3], Greg Easterbrook argues that over the past one hundred years despite remarkable improvements in medicine, science, technology, literature, arts, and any other area that serves to make our lives easier and more comfortable, people aren't happier. In fact, we are arguably more discontent than ever. Easterbrook writes, ". . . the citizens of the United States and the European Union,

---

2. Wayne Grudem, *Christian Ethics: An Introduction to Biblical Moral Reasoning* (Wheaton: Crossway, 2018), 941.

3. Greg Easterbrook, *The Progress Paradox: How Life Gets Better While People Feel Worse* (New York: Random House, 2004). Some of the concrete descriptions selected, along with the kind of illustration I use, is borrowed from Easterbrook, although my illustration is significantly modified.

almost all of whom live better than almost all of the men and women of history, entertain considerable discontent."[4]

You probably know what Easterbrook is talking about. It's common, almost expected, to sense a spirit of ingratitude in conversation with a family or friend. There is an innate feeling in most of us that says we deserve better lives, that what we have now is not enough, and we need a spouse or more money or success to be content. Once I get [fill in the blank], then I'll be happy, we say. You might even feel like God is holding out on you since you currently don't have what you think you need to be content. We read the psalmist's words: "No good thing does he withhold from those who walk uprightly" (Ps. 84:11), and we question the validity of the statement. Jeremiah Burroughs, a seventeenth-century puritan, used the expression "rare jewel" to describe contentment, to illustrate contentment is precious but uncommon. A similar sentiment could be expressed in our day. Despite astonishing progress in almost every area of life over the past century, discontentment abounds.

The Puritans frequently spoke about contentment to help congregants get through common suffering. Life before the twentieth century in most parts of the world, compared to the Western world in which I live, was barbaric. It was not uncommon to die young or to live poor or get a disease or two. Preachers, as a result, proclaimed boldly a message of contentment to help their congregants endure regular seasons of hardship.

Today, the pendulum has swung considerably in the other direction. It's a paradox, I know. But one of the biggest reasons for the widespread discontentment in the world today is precisely *because* of the recent advancements in material prosperity. Nowadays, most in the West don't worry about starving to death. But we do live in an anxious age, and our discontent is caused by our fear of economic decline, social disapproval (both online and in-person), and feeling as if our lives are devoid of meaning and purpose.[5] We have big

---

4. ibid., xvi.
5. Dan Doriani, *Work That Makes a Difference* (Phillipsburg: P&R Publishing, 2021), 39.

dreams, big ambitions, and big desires, and life feels unbearable when they are unfulfilled.

Melissa Kruger gives an illustration of ocean water to teach that God's blessings were never meant to satisfy the deep longings of your soul. If you drink a little bit of ocean water, you'll likely spit it out and it will increase your thirst. But if you drink too much ocean water, you'll die. You were never meant to find satisfaction, to quench your thirst, from ocean water. And yet, the ocean is majestic, isn't it? It's a stunningly beautiful display of God's glory. But problems arise when you try to find in ocean water what it was never created to do for you.[6]

The same is true of material prosperity in relation to personal satisfaction. Before the twentieth century, God's people were discontent when they didn't have material prosperity; God's people today are discontent because we have clung to it too tightly. We're starting to realize that money, comfort, and material goods don't satisfy us as much as we thought they would.

Reasons and Remedies

Most of us currently feel discontentment in some area of life, and, if not now, most likely a season will come soon where it will appear. When we are struggling with discontentment, we don't acknowledge it ourselves or confess it to others because talking about discontentment has a way of making us look like a downer. Perhaps we are not self-aware enough to realize discontentment is the problem of our lives. Over the past several years, it's become easier for us to talk openly about our anxiety and depression. But talking about discontentment makes you feel like the kid sitting by himself at the lunchroom table. We play it down and act like it's not a big deal when it's really killing us on the inside. We feel embarrassed, or we feel shame and guilt, so we hide our discontent

---

6. Quoted in Melissa B. Kruger, *Contentment* (Sanford, FL: Ligonier Ministries, 2018), CD.

or ignore it. But acknowledgment and confession are the paths to healing. Ignoring your discontentment will raise it.

Why are we this way? Why do you struggle with discontentment? Why do I struggle with discontentment? Why do we all struggle with discontentment?

Discontentment is a not a new problem. The reasons for discontentment may be different, and the amount of discontentment we feel may be higher, but the problem of discontentment is as old as the Garden of Eden. The answer for why we struggle with discontentment is complex because people are complex. We are the way we are and we struggle in the ways we do for thousands of reasons. It's impossible to consider all the reasons for both individual and societal discontentment. Nevertheless, discussing common reasons that provoke discontentment promotes self-awareness, helps you to notice the causes when they appear, and sparks ways to fight for contentment when they do.

Secular Media

Some of these practical reasons for discontentment are obvious. One example is advertising. We can broadly categorize this under "secular media." I have two undergraduate business degrees, so I'm well-aware that advertising and media can be done ethically. Done well, the advertising of a product can help solve a need for a consumer.

But ethical advertising does not characterize every advertisement or ad agency.

In an interview with the *Harvard Business Review,* Andrew Oswald, Professor of Economics and Behavioral Science at the University of Warwick in the UK, shares a study that surveyed 900,000 citizens in 27 European countries from 1980 to 2011. The point of the study was to discover if there is a correlation between personal unhappiness and the amount of advertising dollars spent in a particular country. "The higher a country's ad spend was in one year," writes Nicole Torres, a senior editor for the *Harvard Business*

Review, "the less satisfied its citizens were a year or two later." She continues: "Their conclusion: Advertising makes us unhappy."

Oswald reaches the heart level and explains that "exposing people to a lot of advertising raises their aspirations—and makes them feel that their own lives, achievements, belongings, and experiences are inadequate."[7] Advertising makes you feel like all of your desires are needs. But it's not only the advertisements that daily bombard us that prey on our weaknesses to cause discontent, but also the underlying message from society that says we need more money, possessions, and attractiveness if we want social recognition.

Pressure and Expectations

This brings me to a second common reason that propels discontentment: high expectations placed on us from youth. These are the messages delivered to us from family, friends, media, educators, athletes, musicians, and all other culture shapers.[8]

What's the message? Reach for the moon. You can fulfill all of your dreams. You were destined to be a world-changer. You're the captain of your fate, the master of your own soul. For you, the possibilities are endless. You can be anything you want to be when you grow up, as long as you work hard and put your mind to it. Or, even the spiritualized version, "God has big things in store for you." The message that we've heard from youth is that we were meant to be extraordinary, alive to change the world.

Encouragement is a gift. This kind of pep talk can build self-confidence. No one would argue against having a coach in your corner as a source of appropriate comfort. I still remember when my fourth grade P.E. teacher said, "That was awesome, man" in response to my performance in the dreaded one-mile run, even

---

7. Nicole Torres, "Advertising Makes Us Unhappy," *Harvard Business Review,* January/February 2020, https://hbr.org/2020/01/advertising-makes-us-unhappy

8. Robert D. Jones, *Contentment: Joy That Lasts* (Phillipsburg: P&R Publishing, 2019), 23-24.

though I thought I did a terrible job. Teachers and coaches who pull us aside to tell us they believe in us are special.

But, unintentionally, these high expectations placed on us in our youth from people we love or people we admire turn into unrealistic expectations. If we believe these messages embedded in us since adolescence, we begin to have an overly inflated view of our significance. Success becomes an idol. These impossible expectations create self-pressure, and we become unhealthy perfectionists, seeking self-justification through performance. We become self-absorbed, wrongly thinking that life is about us and our success as opposed to rightly thinking that life is about God and his glory. We turn into restless, results-oriented people who seek self-worth in how others perceive us instead of in the God in whose image we were created. These messages may have led J.I. Packer to say, "The world's idea that everyone, from childhood up, should be able at all times to succeed in measurable ways, and that it is a great disgrace not to, hangs over the Christian community like a pall of acrid smoke."[9]

What happens next? We graduate, work ordinary jobs, live life like ordinary Christians, and feel like failures because we realize we probably aren't going to change the world.

You were not created to change the world. You exist for the pleasure and glory of God. You exist to know him and make him known. God's chief end, his main priority, the reason behind everything he does, is to glorify himself. His primary purpose in your life is not to give you a successful life but to work in such a way as to accomplish the goal he has for himself—namely, to glorify himself through you. This is humbling. Life isn't about you. Yet, it's also liberating because it empowers you to live for something bigger and better than yourself.

Proper stewardship (e.g., money, time, spiritual gifts) is essential, and it's good to expect to both see and enjoy fruit from your labor. Godly ambition is good. Christians should be faithful, hard-working stewards. But it's okay to be an ordinary Christian who works

---

9. Quoted in Dave Harvey, *Rescuing Ambition* (Wheaton: Crossway, 2010), 129.

an ordinary job and attends an ordinary church in an ordinary community. The idea that you were created to be extraordinary is a relatively new phenomenon, words that would've been foreign to those living before the twentieth century. Advice received from youth that overexaggerates our place in the world should be filtered with a biblical framework. And then we should redirect our minds to the ultimate mission statement of every Christian: "Man's chief end is to glorify God, and to enjoy him forever."[10]

You were created to be ordinary. If you have some level of influence over others, like a parent or a teacher, let me encourage you not to place unrealistic expectations on those under your charge, but instead to stir them to faithful Christian living.

Options Overload

"I have observed that rather than resulting in excited determination, the number of choices available for activities, relationships, education, and vocation have an overwhelming—at times almost paralysing—effect on young adults' ability to discern a preferable option and pursue it with gratitude and satisfaction,"[11] writes Fran Blomberg, who pleas with young adults to pursue Christian contentment. It's a privilege to have options for school and career choice, but having too many options puts pressure on you to select the right option. Once while eating out with friends, I quickly noticed that the menu was over twenty-five pages long. Unsure about what to choose for lunch, I made a hesitant decision, and sat anxiously once the waiter left, wondering if I made the right decision.

Closely related to having too many options is "opposing forces,"[12] when there's multiple viable options but you can't pick more than one. You want to lose weight, but you also want pizza. You want the new iPhone, but you also need to save money. You want to rise early for private devotions, but you also want to stay up to finish the

---

10. WSC, 1.
11. Fran Blomberg, "Contentment: Radical Discipleship for Young Adults," *Journal of European Baptist Studies* 17:1 (2017), 40.
12. Robert A. Johnson and Jerry M. Ruhl, *Contentment: A Way to True Happiness* (New York: HarperOne, 2000), 101.

movie. This decision-making process creates a sense of FOMO (fear of missing out), and often makes you wonder if you made the right choice, or if you need to be somewhere different or doing something different to be content. The thought that too many options breeds discontentment will make older generations laugh, but it's a crippling issue for many young adults.

Not only do we need growth in personal discipline and the proper stewardship of our emotions, but we also need a robust view of God's sovereignty for all of life. Proverbs 16:33 says, "The lot is cast into the lap, but its every decision is from the Lord." Jesus adds, "Are not two sparrows sold for a penny? And not one of them will fall to the ground apart from your Father" (Matt. 10:29). Even apparently unimportant events like the roll of a dice or a bird hitting the ground don't happen by accident, chance, or luck, but are caused by the triune God who wills everything—good and bad, big and small. If God is active and working to fulfill his plan for humanity even amidst the rolling of a dice or the falling of a bird, how much more active is he for you amidst the setbacks and overlooked details of life? We need a high view of God's sovereignty for both the big decisions of life and the small ones. You've never made a decision that was absent from God's invisible hand.

Digital Media and the Comparison Game

Social media is undoubtedly manufacturing discontentment. When not used purposefully, social media can exploit your heart and foster a spirit of discontentment, partly because of sin, but also because social media companies specifically prey on people with the aim of causing addiction, as told in the engaging documentary, *The Social Dilemma*. Social media addiction makes you discontent. Our insecurities, too, get in the way. We get jealous when others get more likes and shares than we do. Instead of seeking to be useful, we end up comparing ourselves to others, and pathetically try to craft posts to generate likes and followers to boost our self-esteem. And then we feel rejected when our posts don't get a certain amount of attention. We compare our lives to others and assume everyone else has a better life than us.

These are some practical reasons for discontent. But we must go deeper. We must discuss sin and our hearts.

Your Restless Heart

We are sinners because we are discontent; we are discontent because we are sinners.

For centuries, the Church has used the triad of *the world, the flesh, and the devil* to broadly categorize the origin of temptation. This framework helps us understand why discontentment is so pervasive. "The world" in Scripture is often used to describe the sinful behavior and corrupt values of an unbelieving culture. The flesh, on the other hand, is equated with desire. It comes to mind when we ponder James' words, "But each person is tempted when he is lured and enticed by his own desire" (James 1:14). The word desire is the same word Paul uses for "to covet" when he says, "For I would not have known what it is to covet if the law had not said, 'You shall not covet'" (Rom. 7:7). Discontentment occurs when we inordinately desire something we presently don't have. Finally, the demonic forces of evil provoke discontentment: "The devil prowls around like a roaring lion, seeking someone to devour" (1 Pet. 5:8). Satan and his servants want you to believe that the path to obtain contentment is through sin.

But the big, primary, underlying reason we are discontent is because we have failed to love God with our whole hearts and to love our neighbors as ourselves. Discontentment is the result of failing to love God and neighbor correctly.

Usually, people seek contentment through either detachment or accumulation. Detachment is emotional withdrawal to avoid dealing with the mess of life, and accumulation believes that more pleasure and possessions will create contentment. It's not healthy to live in denial and it's incorrect to assume that acquiring more pleasure or possessions will make you content. Augustine, a theologian and early church father, spoke about sin in terms of "disordered loves."

We sin when we love anything more than God. It's when we look to sex, marriage, children, and success to fulfill us. It's when we expect created things to give us what they were never created to give. God and God alone can satisfy the deepest longings of your heart. So we must love God first and foremost. Pursuing Christian contentment is not about not loving anything but about loving God *more* than anything. When we do, everything seems to fall into place, and, slowly but surely, contentment arrives. This is why Augustine famously said, "Our hearts are restless until they find rest in you." Loving God means loving him with your whole heart and loving him for him, not for what he can give you, but simply for who he is, for his glorious attributes and actions. Only when our hearts are transformed by God's love for us in Christ can we love him more than we love anything else.[13]

Sin is not just against God but also against our neighbor. Contentment derives from loving God more, but also by treating others better. We must love our neighbors as ourselves and fervently practice the golden rule (Matt. 7:12). So often in relationships we seek what we can get. We seek affirmation. We seek leveraging our networks to advance our career. We see others as primarily what they can do for us. Like Jesus who came to serve, and not to be served (Mark 10:45), we should take the posture of a servant in relationships. We'll enjoy our relationships more when we treat people with value and respect as opposed to treating people as a means to further our self-interests.

Counterfeit Contentment

As is often the case with big issues like discontentment, there are many proposed solutions to the problem.

1. **The Tips and Tricks Approach.** This kind of material appears in a "Ten Things Every Person in the World Should Know about Contentment (Especially #2)" article. The advice is pithy, tweetable, and immediately actionable. Those who advocate The Tips and

---

13. Tim Keller, *Making Sense of God: An Invitation to the Skeptical* (New York: Penguin Books, 2018), 77-96.

Tricks Approach will tell you to choose your words wisely and to write down three blessings you're grateful for every day. Want to be content? Watch your diet. Learn to live with fewer choices. Shorten your commute, lower your stress, reduce your debt, spend more time with friends and family. Tips and Tricks evangelists love to tell people to cheer up and look on the bright side and remember that there's always tomorrow. If you desire contentment, what you really need to do is sit down in a scenic place, take a few deep breaths, quiet the noise in your mind, and listen. To what? Nobody knows, but you might hear a voice if you try hard enough. While you're sitting there, place your hand on your heart, take several deep breaths, and think of something touchy-feely. And as you sit there, remember: the grass is greener on the other side. Or better yet, where you water it.

God has given talent and wisdom to all people, so we can learn from everyone. Take, for example, the idea of writing down three things you're grateful for every day. This beloved habit is practiced daily by many Christians. Often, keeping a gratitude journal elevates the noticeability of God's mercies in your life. There is value in common sense advice like finding a shorter commute and reducing your debt.

But the problem with The Tips and Tricks Approach is that God is replaced with self. It assumes you can manufacture contentment through personal effort alone. But you can't. You can't experience contentment without God's help. Remove God and you have no chance of true, lasting contentment.

With The Tips and Tricks Approach, whatever amount of minimal contentment you get won't last. Making changes to your external environment to experience contentment only works temporarily. You might have a better day or two. Or maybe even a better month. The advice from The Tips and Tricks Approach temporarily provides a better outlook on life, but fails as a long-term solution. Not only is this method exhausting, but the rewards are minimal. Without grace-driven effort *in conjunction* with empowerment from God, attempts at contentment are in vain.

2. **The Stoic Approach.** Stoicism is "a real or pretended indifference to pleasure or pain."[14] Emotion is severely minimized. Stoics focus on controlling desires through logic, self-denial, and teeth-gritting effort. This method advocates detaching yourself emotionally from people or possessions to find resources within yourself to manage life with tranquility. Stoics fear being exposed or perceived as weak. To avoid unhappiness from changing circumstances, don't love anything too much. Through self-mastery, you can achieve contentment. It's a philosophy designed to increase resilience, happiness and virtue—all through independence.

Interestingly, stoicism is presently growing in popularity. The logic of stoicism is endorsed by widely recognized self-help gurus who morph stoicism with self-help advice with the aim of helping others take personal responsibility for their success.

As an independent person who is much more of a thinker than a feeler, stoicism seems appealing. The idea of gritting through life through sheer rationale intrigues me because I love the life of the mind. I bet I could get decently far as a stoic, say, for a year or two. But eventually, I would break down and fall apart. That's because stoicism sets you up for a crushing blow. Stoicism dehumanizes the human soul because it undermines the fact that humans are made in God's image (Gen. 1:27). It promotes self-restraint for self-exaltation. It connects your self-worth to your personal achievements. It doesn't teach you to properly handle your emotions.

Humans are emotional beings. It's not healthy to continually ignore your emotions to bear life. Part of living in the *imago dei* (Latin for "image of God") is to be men and women who appropriately process and steward our emotions. God himself cannot change and will never feel a sinful emotion, but he is the origin and creator of emotions[15]—the one who loves, grieves, and rejoices.

---

14. *American Dictionary of the English Language*, 82.
15. Wayne Grudem, *Systematic Theology: An Introduction to Biblical Doctrine*, *first edition* (Grand Rapids: Zondervan, 1994), 166.

"Only love of the immutable brings tranquility,"[16] says Augustine. Contentment, or tranquility, doesn't come through intentionally ignoring your feelings through life's many changes, but in loving the God who never changes. In the end, stoicism fails to provide lasting contentment and will harden your heart, leading to bitterness, cynicism and self-righteousness.

3. **The Never Enough Approach.** I remember a time during college when I was sitting around a table with a bunch of football players eating lunch and talking about future life accomplishments. One player in particular was adamant about accomplishing several goals. After giving his mini-motivational speech about why we should never settle, he looked me dead in the eye and said, "We should never be content in life, right, David?"

The Never Enough Approach views contentment as a weakness, and this attitude toward contentment is fairly new. Before the twentieth century's technological advances that led to unprecedented prosperity in the world, contentment was esteemed highly in culture, literature, arts, technology, theology and especially, philosophy.[17] For most of the history of the world, life was cruel, characterized by tragedy and sorrow, so pursuing contentment made sense to navigate through life. But now? With the life expectancy drastically higher than it's ever been and with more opportunities for fortune and fame than ever, contentment has been trivialized, now seen as something to avoid. Contentment is overlooked, underappreciated, and countercultural.

No people group exemplifies a distaste for contentment more than Never Enough advocates. They believe contentment is a sign you're not maximizing your potential. It's impossible to have too much money and success. You can always be working harder, always accomplishing more goals. Their lives are defined by phrases like "Never Settle" and "No Days Off" and "Whatever it Takes." Ambitious people are

---

16. Quoted in Tim Keller, *Walking with God in Pain and Suffering* (New York: Penguin Random House, 2015), 387.

17. Richard Swenson, *Contentment: The Secret to Lasting Calm* (Colorado Springs: NavPress, 2013), 75.

particularly prone to adopt this method. They are hungry, restless and driven.

Those who embrace the Never Enough Approach are the hardest working people you'll ever find. They rightly understand that life is short and they try to make every day count. Usually, those who adopt The Never Enough Approach are the ones who soar in their occupations and leave a dent in this world.

They also leave dents in their souls. They avoid life's two biggest questions: (1) Why am I here? (2) What happens to me after I die? That's because they ignore their conscience. They keep themselves busy and full of goals and distractions to spare themselves from thinking about questions pertaining to the meaning of life. History is not short of examples of people who tried filling their lives with an endless amount of pleasure, only to leave them feeling emptier than when their original quest for world dominance began.

The Bible not only encourages contentment but *commands* it (Heb. 13:5). To speak poorly about contentment is to go against Scripture and ultimately against God. If you ignore God's wisdom and try to live life through self-made rules, you may feel autonomous and happy at first, but in due time you'll ruin your life trying to find joy in worldly achievements alone. For apart from God, who can find contentment?

Think about King Solomon from Ecclesiastes. He built great works and houses and vineyards and gardens and parks and fruit trees and pools (Eccles. 2:4-6). He had servants and more possessions and herds than anyone who ever lived in his country, surpassing them all in greatness (Eccles. 2:7-9). He was mega-rich (Eccles. 2:8). He hired people to sing to him (Eccles. 2:8). He had lots of concubines (Eccles. 2:8). He got whatever he wanted with zero restraint (Eccles. 2:10). His conclusion to his efforts? "Then I considered all that my hands had done and the toil I had expended in doing it, and behold, all was vanity and a striving after wind . . ." (Eccles. 2:11). His conclusion on the meaning of life? "The end of the matter; all has been heard. Fear God and keep his commandments, for this is the whole duty of man" (Eccles. 12:13).

We don't need to test the waters of sinful pleasure to see if they produce contentment or not. We have a million examples in history and a few dozen in Scripture that show us they won't. No Christ-follower should ever feel like an unrepentant sinful lifestyle is better than the Christian one. You can take it from Solomon, or you can take it from former NFL Quarterback Tom Brady who, after winning his third Super Bowl ring, infamously said, "Why do I have three Super Bowl rings, and still think there's something greater out there for me?"[18] Never Enough people are always striving but never satisfied.

4. **The Hyper-Spiritual Approach.** You pretend that you're content when you're not and you masquerade your discontent through hyper-spiritual God-talk. This approach is keen on reflexively using expressions like "I'm content in all circumstances" or "I'm just waiting on the Lord" when trusted friends and family inquire about an area of particular pain. It's obviously good to wait on the Lord. Some people who use these statements in response to questions about an enduring trial are being genuine. But some Christians use spiritual language to hide their discontent. We feel bad for struggling with discontentment and we don't know how to process or talk about our emotions. We want to seem further along in our spiritual journey than we are.

Spiritually "faking it" is exhausting. It's okay to have doubts, fears, struggles and questions; we should share them with the Lord in prayer and selectively share them with trusted Christian friends. We should ask God to surround us with godly mentors and friends with whom we can share the messy parts of our lives. As you grow in Christ, you'll eventually accept that uncomfortable feeling of exposure when sharing your life with trusted friends, knowing that the people you open up to genuinely love you and are ready to help

---

18. Daniel Schorn, "Transcript: Tom Brady, Part 3," November 4th, 2005, https://www.cbsnews.com/news/transcript-tom-brady-part-3/

bear your burdens (Gal. 6:2). Every Christian should have at least one person in their life with whom they can share anything.

The four commonly suggested solutions mentioned above don't solve the problem of discontentment but only raise it. We still need a better, more reliable remedy for our discontentment.

Where do we turn?

What Contentment Doesn't Mean

Troubled. That's how Jesus felt on a few occasions during his earthly ministry: "Now is my soul troubled" (John 12:27). And again, "After saying these things, Jesus was troubled in his spirit" (John 13:21). The word "troubled" means to be unsettled, stirred up, full of inward turmoil. It conveys horror and revulsion,[19] and is "a word that is often used of people when they are anxious or suddenly very surprised by danger."[20] A similar usage of the word is found in Psalm 6:3 when the psalmist says: "My soul is in deep *anguish*. How long, Lord, how long?" (NIV). And again in Psalm 42:5: "Why are you cast down, O my soul, and why are you in *turmoil* within me?" Jesus, the God-man, the only person in the history of the world who never sinned and was perfectly content, felt troubled.

Jesus was troubled because it was the last week of his life and he knew that he would soon be beaten beyond recognition, bear the wrath of God, and die a brutal death on a blood-stained tree. This is similar to what he felt in the Garden of Gethsemane where he was in such anguish that his sweat became like drops of blood (Luke 22:44). The full humanity of Jesus is on display. He has emotions. He feels deeply. Sorrow and contentment are not incompatible. It's possible to be simultaneously troubled and content.

A quick glance at the life and ministry of Jesus shows he got angry (John 2:13-17), annoyed with people (Matt. 17:17), rebuked

---

19. D.A. Carson, *The Gospel According to John* (Grand Rapids: Eerdmans, 1990), 440.

20. Wayne Grudem, *Systematic Theology, Second Edition, An Introduction to Biblical Doctrine* (Grand Rapids: Zondervan Academic, 2020), 667.

the religious leaders (Matt. 23:1-36), and even made a request to his Father to remove the cup of wrath (Luke 22:42), a way of asking if there could be another way for God's wrath to be satisfied. Anger, annoyance, a rebuke, a request. All emotions or actions that are not incongruent with contentment.

Contentment doesn't mean passivity or laziness. It doesn't mean inactivity or emotionally checking out. We tend to chalk up people who are laid back and mellow as models of contentment. Maybe they are, or perhaps they are people who neglect responsibility. Contentment doesn't mean complacency. Our work should be defined by excellence since we want to do everything for God's glory (1 Cor. 10:31). Contentment is also not masochism (deriving pleasure from pain) or fatalism (withdrawing because everything is determined by fate). The contented life is not incompatible with dreams, goals, and desires.

You can be loud and outgoing and a bit dramatic and still be content. Although some people will find contentment more difficult because of genetics or difficult circumstances or personal trauma, Christian contentment is not a personality trait; it's not something determined by your natural temperament or wiring.

Okay, then *what* is contentment?

Defining Contentment

The word "content" appears six times[21] in the New Testament, and the word "contentment," once.[22] It's used as a noun (1 Tim. 6:6), an adjective (Phil. 4:11), and a verb (Luke 3:14). In the New Testament original language, the word for contentment is *autárkeia* ("ar-tar-kay-ah"). Strictly speaking, it means "self-

---

21. Luke 3:14, 1 Timothy 6:8, Hebrews 13:5, 3 John 1:10, 2 Corinthians 12:10, Philippians 4:11.

22. 1 Timothy 6:6. However, the same Greek word that Paul uses for "contentment" in 1 Timothy 6:6 is also the same word for "sufficiency" in 2 Corinthians 9:8 where Paul writes, "And God is able to make all grace abound to you, so that having all *sufficiency* in all things at all times, you may abound in every good work." Contentment and a sense of sufficiency go together.

sufficiency."[23] Christian contentment means you feel a sense of sufficiency. It means you have what you need and more: you have more than enough. Appropriate synonyms for contentment are happiness, fulfillment and satisfaction.

A leading English dictionary says contentment is "rest or quietness of the mind in the present condition; satisfaction which holds the mind in peace, restraining complaint, opposition, or further desire, and often implying a moderate degree of happiness."[24] Good start. But not distinctly Christian.

Probably the best definition of Christian contentment comes from Jeremiah Burroughs. In his book, *The Rare Jewel of Christian Contentment*, Burroughs says "Christian contentment is that sweet, inward, quiet, gracious frame of spirit, which freely submits to and delights in God's wise and fatherly disposal in every condition."[25]

Let's define Christian contentment as follows:

Christian contentment: the freedom from dependence on desired circumstances that comes from God's empowering grace to endure everything with rejoicing.

In other words:

- **The freedom from dependence on desired circumstances.** You may desire a change of circumstances, but you're not dependent on them. Your happiness doesn't derive from external sources. A change of circumstances doesn't sway you either too greatly up or down. You're level-headed, even-keeled, and not continually dominated by emotions.
- **God's empowering grace.** You can't experience true, lasting contentment through your own strength. What separates a Christian understanding of contentment from a secular one is the emphasis on God's grace as both empowering (Phil. 4:13)

---

23. Arndt, W., Danker, F. W., Bauer, W., & Gingrich, F. W., *A Greek-English Lexicon of the New Testament and Other Early Christian Literature* (Chicago: University of Chicago Press., 2000), 152.
24. *American Dictionary of the English Language*, 47.
25. Burroughs, *Rare Jewel*, 19.

and sufficient (2 Cor. 12:9) to endure any situation. You're not dependent on your circumstances, but you are dependent on God.

- **Rejoicing.** The Apostle Paul commands us to "Rejoice in the Lord always..." (Phil. 4:4). I take the word "rejoice" and "always" to mean in every situation of life. Rejoicing is not restricted to a feeling. It doesn't mean you'll constantly feel an emotional high. Rejoicing, instead, means to make yourself glad in God, leading to an inward confidence of God's sovereignty and goodness in all situations.

My definition of contentment derives in part from a Bible dictionary, where the editors say that contentment:

"... denotes freedom from reliance upon others, whether other persons or other things; hence the satisfaction of one's needs (2 Cor. 9:8), or the control of one's desires (1 Tim. 6:6, 8). It is not a passive acceptance of the *status quo*, but the positive assurance that God has supplied one's needs, and the consequent release from unnecessary desire. The Christian can be 'self-contained' because he has been satisfied by the grace of God (2 Cor. 12:9). The Christian Spirit of contentment follows ... supremely the example and teaching of Jesus, who rebuked the discontent which grasps at material possessions to neglect of God (Lk. 12:13-21) and who commended such confidence in our father in heaven as will dispel all anxiety concerning physical supplies."[26]

Understanding Contentment

Discontentment is not all bad. There is a right kind of discontentment, what you might call a holy discontent. It is right to feel frustration when God's glory is minimized. It is right to continually pursue knowledge of God, not being satisfied with the knowledge you already have. It is right to feel a burning desire for lost people to come to Christ. Holy discontent is a sign of a healthy Christian. By

---

26. I. Howard Marshalll, A. R. Millard, J.I. Packer, and D.J. Wiseman, eds., *New Bible Dictionary* (Downers Grove: IVP Academic, 1996), 222.

contrast, the sin of discontentment—not being satisfied in God—is the cause of many issues in our personal lives and society today.

What else is there to say about contentment? Contentment is *"being satisfied and at peace with God's will in all situations."*[27] It's an inward state of satisfaction regardless of circumstances. It's characterized by inward peace and joy. Contentment is not about what happens to you, but what's going on inside of you. The quality of our lives is less about what happens to us and more about how we *respond* to what happens to us, and you won't respond well if you're not content. Contentment is a skill, like a jump shot in basketball. It requires practice and effort. It doesn't stick like glue; it builds like knowledge. It's something you can improve. And although contentment is attainable, it's slippery. You may think contentment is firm in your grasp, and then suddenly it diminishes, or even vanishes. It's something you must continually pursue and protect.

In theology talk, the aseity of God refers to God's self-sufficiency. God is not dependent on creation and did not create the world for personal need. Jonathan Edwards states, "It is evident, by both Scripture and reason, that God is infinitely, eternally, unchangeably, and independently glorious and happy."[28] Although we cannot reflect God's aseity since we are by nature dependent creatures, spiritual flourishing derives from reflecting God's character. Contentment, then, is also a virtue. It's a character trait to cultivate godliness. For when you are content in God, you mirror the God who himself is always perfectly content. Few characteristics oppose God's character more than discontentment.

You have to see the value of contentment. Typically, if we think something is valuable, we are willing to sacrifice to obtain it. Learning contentment will alleviate anxiety, satisfy your soul, remove impatience, improve your well-being, and give you a deep inner sense of peace and joy. Contentment makes you calm, cool and collected on the inside, even if there are raging storms of trials in

---

27. Dave Harvey, *Rescuing Ambition*, 123.
28. Quoted in Jonathan Edwards's essay, *A Dissertation Concerning the End for Which God Created the World.*

your life on the outside. It will give you a sense of stability through the ups and downs of life. It's also evangelistic. Christians who are content amid suffering or prosperity set a good example for the watching world. You'll also be edifying your Christian friends because godliness is attractive.

Contentment is simple to understand but hard to live out.[29] Knowing that contentment is possible and valuable, well, that's the easy part. Living it out? Not so much. Contentment is a lifelong process, a long-term and long haul investment. Through knowledge and practice and effort and God's supernatural power, you can grow in contentment over time. Any effort to pursue contentment is worth it.

But how? I'll tell you. But first, let me ask you some questions.

---

29. Megan Hill, *Contentment: Seeing God's Goodness* (Phillipsburg: P&R, 2018), 11.

Chapter 2
Signs and Symptoms

"Oh, the temptation that men of discontented spirits are subject to! The devil loves to fish in troubled waters." — Jeremiah Burroughs

The root of all sin is discontentment. Discontentment, to borrow an illustration from Puritan Thomas Watson, is a mother sin that gives birth to other sins. Your discontentment leads to unrighteous anger which leads to yelling at your child which leads to a personal wound —and it all started with discontent. Discontentment is vertical (sin against God), horizontal (sin against neighbor), and personal (self-inflicting). Everyone in your life loses when you're discontent.

Puritan Thomas Boston referred to discontent as a "hellish" sin. When we think of sins deserving of hell, we often think of the most vile sins committed by the most wicked people. But we label discontent as a small sin and assume it's not *that* bad. Some Christians don't marvel at God's grace because they don't understand the severity of sin. Some of us have unknowingly undermined God's holiness.

The culture is catechizing you. This is especially true if you spend significant time on social media or watching television. Secular marketing ads promote self-worship. "You deserve it," is a core message. Of course, the goal of this message is to get you to spend money, like on an expensive new outfit or exotic vacation. But the secular catechizing in media communications subconsciously creates entitlement and minimizes the nature of sin. Being catechized by the culture makes it difficult to see what we truly deserve: eternal condemnation. Our Savior has rescued us from God's wrath forever, but our discontentment sent our Savior to the cross. We won't be serious about killing the sin of discontentment until we understand how habitual discontent provokes God's displeasure. It is a hellish sin.

Conventional wisdom states that pride is the root of all sin. There is, therefore, a direct link between pride and discontentment. But there are other signs and symptoms to detect discontent. What are they? Here are five of them:

- Worry
- Coveting
- Grumbling
- Unrighteous anger
- Unhealthy dwelling

Although this list is suggestive and not exhaustive, these five symptoms in question format below will spark healthy introspection. Answering these questions honestly will help you better understand where and why you struggle with discontent.

Evil Opponents of Christian Contentment: Five Questions

I. Do I struggle with grumbling?

Constant grumbling is the number one sign of a discontented person.

Lament, doubt, and anguished prayer are part of what it means to live Christianly in a fallen world. When doubting Thomas said that he wouldn't believe in the resurrection of Jesus unless he saw and placed his fingers into the mark of the nails on Jesus' hands, Jesus didn't scold him, but allowed Thomas to do so, urging him to believe (John 20:24-29). When Nathaniel wondered: "Can anything good come out of Nazareth?" Jesus, knowing Nathaniel spoke ill of his hometown, replied: "Behold, an Israelite indeed, in whom there is no deceit!" (John 1:47). God cares about the doubts, fears and questions of his people.

The Psalms are filled with raw emotion: "O God, why do you cast us off forever?" (Ps. 74:1a). Although the line between grumbling and lament is blurry, the psalmists aren't afraid to be honest with God. You too should sprint to God in prayer when under distress in order to discharge any and all feelings, concerns, and requests that you have (1 Pet. 5:7). As it's been said, perhaps the difference between lament (not-sinful) and grumbling (sinful) is that, with lament, you complain *to* God; with grumbling, you complain about God. Occasionally grumble? You're human. But if you habitually grumble, you have a heart issue to examine.

No other account in Scripture reveals the hatred God feels toward grumbling more than when the Israelites moved from Egypt to the Promised Land. In Egypt the Israelites were slaves. Economically, they were oppressed. Part of their religious freedom was denied. They were afflicted with heavy burdens (Exod. 1:11) and their lives were characterized by oppression and grueling toil (Exod. 1:14). They were under tyrannical leadership and lacked provision; they feared for their lives.

And then God steps in: "And God heard their groaning, and God remembered his covenant with Abraham, with Isaac, and with Jacob. God saw the people of Israel—and God knew" (Exod. 2:24-25). Through a series of dramatic and supernatural events, God miraculously rescues the Israelites from slavery, foreshadowing the act of redemption that takes place for all who trust in Christ. The Israelites walk on water when God parts the Red Sea and they eventually arrive in the Promised Land to enjoy fellowship with God as their covenant Lord.

But then within one month of leaving Egypt, something terrible happens. The Israelites begin to grumble: "And the whole congregation of the people of Israel grumbled against Moses and Aaron in the wilderness, and the people of Israel said to them, 'Would that we had died by the hand of the Lord in the land of Egypt, when we sat by the meat pots and ate bread to the full, for you have brought us out into this wilderness to kill this whole assembly with hunger'" (Exod. 16:2-3).

The Israelites grumble about food (Num. 11:4-6) and water (Exod. 15:24). Moses grumbles about the people God entrusted him to lead (Num. 11:10-15). Miriam and Aaron grumble against Moses (Num. 12:1). The Israelites grumble about the battles that stand between them and the Promised Land (Num. 13:28-29). They also grumble about their hardships and the leadership of Moses (Num. 14:1-14).

God is patient, and he demonstrates his patience toward his people through provision. Despite the Israelites' unfaithfulness, God provides them with manna and quail, and sweetens the bitter waters (Exod. 15:22-25). But God's patience is limited, and he does not feel indifferent toward habitual grumbling: "How long shall this wicked congregation grumble against me? I have heard the grumblings of the people of Israel, which they grumble against me. Say to them, 'As I live, declares the LORD, what you have said in my hearing I will do to you: your dead bodies shall fall in this wilderness, and of all your number, listed in the census from twenty years old and upward, who have grumbled against me" (Num. 14:26-29). The plague kills over 14,000+ Israelites (Num. 16:49). "We must not . . . ," the Apostle Paul writes, hundreds of years later, "grumble, as some of them did and were destroyed by the Destroyer" (1 Cor. 10:10). A person might protest that's the God of the Old Testament, but the God of the Old Testament is the God who never changes (Heb. 13:8). It's alarming how much God hates when his people regularly grumble about their circumstances.

Jude writes that one day Jesus will come back to "execute judgment" on the "grumblers" and "malcontents" (see Jude 14-16). Malcontent means complaining about your lot in life. You might expect Jude to say, "Jesus is coming back to execute judgment on all unrepentant murderers and abusive people." But "grumblers" and "malcontents" top the list: "These are grumblers, malcontents, following their own sinful desires; they are loud-mouthed boasters, showing favoritism to gain advantage" (Jude 1:16).

Grumbling is the action, but what's the heart issue of grumbling? Idolatry, usually. Grumbling is a worship issue. When we grumble, we pronounce a theological statement; we're admitting we don't truly believe God is good and has our best in mind. Grumbling reveals your idols. Where your grumbling is, there your idols will be also.

We consider ourselves mature Christians because we are sexually faithful and don't have alcohol problems, but we conveniently overlook the habitual spirit of grumbling in our lives, as if it's not a big spiritual problem.

Here's good news: Those in Christ will never experience the eternal wrath of God. We've been rescued forever from eternal condemnation. Yes, and amen. But it's incorrect to assume that we can now express any attitude and commit any action we desire and expect only God's blessing because we are in Christ. No, we are saved from God's wrath in order to live lives of holiness. Christians incur God's Fatherly chastisement through ongoing and unrepentant disobedience. So we live with joy and peace, knowing our greatest need in life has been covered by God, but we strive for obedience until the Lord comes back or calls us home. Knowing that we are free from God's eternal wrath, but can still receive God's Fatherly discipline, should not lead to paranoia and unhealthy fear, but instead motivate godly living.

People say our actions spring from our character. True. But what's equally true is that your actions affect your character.[1] Grumbling is the result of a character deficiency, but grumbling also makes your character worse. What you do is the result of who you are, but what you do determines who you will become. In his commentary on Proverbs, Derek Kidner, the late Old Testament scholar, says, "Superficial habits of talk react on the mind; so that, e.g., cynical chatter, fashionable grumbles, flippancy, half-truths, barely meant in the first place, harden into well-established habits of thought."[2]

---

1. Thank you to Dr. John Collins for this insight.
2. Derek Kidner, *Proverbs* (Westmont: IVP Academic, 2018), 65.

Let's not speed pass what Kidner says. The little remarks you make on a regular basis form the kind of person you will become.

The more you complain, the more tempted you will be to complain and the less of an issue it will seem to you.

2. Do I struggle with coveting?

Eve, the only person in history who lived in a perfect place (Eden) and had a perfect spouse (Adam), still wasn't content.[3]

Jerry Krause was the general manager of the Chicago Bulls from 1985 to 2003. A shrewd businessman who made millions, Krause assembled one of the best NBA basketball teams in history. But he had one big problem. Krause suffered with jealousy and envy, which in part ended the dominant run by the Bulls, an account told in the thrilling documentary, *The Last Dance.* As Michael Jordan and the Chicago Bulls won championships and dominated professional basketball for nearly a decade, Krause was hurt because he did not get the attention he felt he deserved for assembling the team. Instead of enjoying the team's success, Krause worked behind the scenes to end one of basketball's most historic franchises. What could possibly lead a person to tear down an organization he helped build and crush the sport's dreams of millions of international fans? Envy.[4]

Coveting is an excessive desire to have something you don't currently have. Or, as John Piper says, "Covetousness is desiring something so much that you lose your contentment in God."[5] Eve's *desire* for the forbidden fruit was sinful, not just eating it. You know you're struggling with jealousy or coveting when you're willing to sin to obtain something you don't presently have, and when you feel satisfaction when you learn of a failure of someone's life you envy. We may say, "I covet your prayers," but "coveting" is not a positive term. Coveting is a grave sin, so much so that Paul says that the one who is "covetous has no inheritance in the kingdom of God"

---

3.   This is a common observation made by various writers on contentment.

4.   https://www.sportsmockery.com/chicago-bulls/last-dance-reveals-how-hated-jerry-krause-was-in-bulls-locker-room/

5.   John Piper, *Future Grace, Revised Edition: The Purifying Power of the Promises of God* (Colorado Springs: Multnomah, 2012), 221.

(Eph. 5:5). Elsewhere he puts coveting on a list of sins such as sexual immorality (Col. 3:5). Envy, what Augustine referred to as the sin of the devil, is a major sign of discontentment.

One of the Bible's most significant teachings on coveting is the tenth commandment: "You shall not covet your neighbor's house; you shall not covet your neighbor's wife, or his male servant, or his female servant, or his ox, or his donkey, or anything that is your neighbor's" (Exod. 20:17). This commandment starts specifically: neighbor's house, wife, male servant or female servant, ox or donkey. And ends generally: "or anything that is your neighbor's." The tenth commandment doesn't forbid desire or acquisition; it forbids setting your heart on what God has not provided.

The ten commandments are deeper than most Christians realize. Consider these two catechism questions[6]:

1. **Q**: What is required in the tenth commandment?
    A: Full **contentment** with our condition, with a right and charitable frame of spirit toward our neighbor, and all that is his.
2. **Q**: What is forbidden in the tenth commandment?
    A: All **discontentment** with our own estate, envying or grieving at the good of our neighbor, and all inordinate motions and affections to anything that is his.

Each commandment not only promotes certain actions and desires, but also prohibits certain actions and desires. In Scripture, whenever we're told what not to do, there is an implication of something God wants us to do (and vice versa). Notice what the two catechism questions teach: contentment (what God wants) is required, but discontentment (what God doesn't want) is forbidden. You can't be content and covetous simultaneously.

---

6. WSC, questions 80 and 81, slightly edited, emphasis mine.

Where are some areas where we may struggle with envy? Here are some examples:[7]

- Romantic relationships
- Money and possessions
- Talent, gifts and abilities
- Beauty and attractiveness
- Opportunities and success
- Seasons and circumstances
- Friends and familial relationships

Fundamentally, coveting stems from unbelief. It's wrong because it distrusts both God's provision and God's wisdom. Distrusting God's provision believes God's provision is inadequate; distrusting God's wisdom believes God's will is incorrect. Coveting overexaggerates the good others have received and minimizes the good we have received. It fixates on what you don't have. It reveals that God is not the greatest and most satisfying reality in our lives. It falsely believes you need something other than God to satisfy the deep longings of your soul. It's destructive because so much of being a happy person in a fallen world comes from enjoying God's provision in the moment.

How can we tell if we are envious? Consider these four ways from Melissa Kruger, along with examples[8]:

1. The object of our desire is wrong [you desire someone else's husband or wife].
2. The means to go about obtaining our desire is wrong [you're willing to marry an unbeliever].
3. The motivation for our desire is wrong [you long for marriage because you think it will complete you].
4. The attitude while waiting for our desire is wrong [you constantly grumble about your singleness].

---

7. Largely adapted from Melissa Kruger, *The Envy of Eve: Finding Contentment in a Covetous World* (Fearn, Ross-Shire: Christian Focus Publications, 2012), 15-16.
8. Adapted from Melissa Kruger, *The Envy of Eve*, 36.

Coveting leads to many sins, even murder: "You desire and do not have, so you murder" (James 4:2). Nobody has ever been sentenced to prison for coveting, but coveting has led to many felonies. Eve coveted, and her sin was passed down to her son Cain, who murdered Abel. Rachel said, "Give me children, or I shall die!" (Gen. 30:1). Rachel has children, but then dies in childbirth. Consider why Pontius Pilate sentenced Jesus to be crucified: "For he knew that it was out of envy that they had delivered him up" (Matt. 27:18). Think about how much more satisfied your life would be if you ceased coveting: "A tranquil heart gives life to the flesh, but envy makes the bones rot" (Prov. 14:30). Contentment is life-giving; envy produces pain. We cannot consider ourselves mature Christians until we are able to rejoice with those who rejoice (Rom. 12:15).

In the end, envy happens when we notice how God has blessed others but forget how God has blessed us. If comparison is the *thief* of joy, then contentment is the *chief* of joy. We can choose to compare. Or we can choose to give thanks.

3. Do I struggle with unrighteous anger?

Is anger always sinful? No. There's a difference between righteous anger and unrighteous anger, just like there's a difference between murder and authorized killings. Murder is always a sin, but some killings are justifiable, like self-defense, just war and capital punishment. In the Old Testament, some killings were justifiable because God's law was continually disregarded. After displaying patience for a time, God executed either individuals or whole communities, a prerogative reserved for God and God alone. Similarly, righteous anger is permissible. The Bible never says, "Thou shall not get angry." Instead, Paul teaches, "Be angry and do not sin . . ." (Eph. 4:26). So we must differentiate between righteous and unrighteous anger.

Righteous anger is geared toward sin, injustice and oppression. Never feel anger? That's not good. It's a blessing not to struggle with unrighteous anger as a besetting sin, but what makes God angry should also make you angry. Never getting angry might be a sign of passivity, coldness and indifference. Your lack of anger could be indicative of a lack of love. High school bullying makes me angry, which aligns with the heart of God who himself hates oppression. Unrighteous anger is all other forms of anger. In particular, Jesus rebukes unjustifiable anger directed toward those in Christ (Matt. 5:21-24).

Going back to the commandments, the sixth commandment is against murder. When Jesus added to the severity of this commandment in his Sermon on the Mount (Matt. 5:21-22), he teaches that just because you haven't physically committed murder doesn't mean you haven't violated the sixth commandment. Unrighteous anger in your heart is also sinful. Violation of the sixth commandment also includes racism, hatred, abortion, and the desire to seek revenge, all of which stem from unrighteous anger, all of which reveal discontentment.

Anger doesn't look the same for everyone. When we think of angry people, we think of verbally or physically abusive drunks. True. But this is only one form. Anger is a multi-headed monster with many disgusting facial expressions. A passive-aggressive person, for example, is angry. They lack the inward security to have a confrontational conversation, so they go behind your back to hurt you.

Most unrighteous anger comes down to an aspiration to be sovereign over the universe. It's when we put ourselves in the position of God and expect that our expectations should always be met and people should always act according to our desires. The next time you get angry over something silly, ask yourself why you're getting angry. Look closely, and you might be unpleasantly surprised to discover your anger is directed toward something you are trusting for your identity.

4. Do I struggle with non-clinical worry or anxiety?

Mental health issues are real. I'm thankful for the increased awareness to mental health over the past two decades. When I mention worry and anxiety (or any related mental health issue), I'm not talking about the clinical kind that results from genetics or trauma. It's undeniably true that some Christians are plagued with severe, clinical anxiety and may need medication and professional counseling, both of which I advocate. I'm not talking about the kind of anxiety we can't control but the kind that Jesus and Paul discuss: sinful anxiety stemming from distrust of God (Matt. 6:25-34; Phil. 4:4-7).

Jesus says, "Therefore I tell you, do not be anxious about your life, what you will eat or what you will drink, nor about your body, what you will put on. Is not life more than food, and the body more than clothing?" (Matt. 6:25). The immediate context is money because that's what Jesus discusses in the previous verses (Matt. 6:19-24). But we are weak and prone to worry about everything. Jesus isn't promoting carelessness or laziness. Worry about provision is forbidden, not responsible work habits.

Contemplate the human-animal distinction: "Look at the birds of the air: they neither sow nor reap nor gather into barns, and yet your heavenly Father feeds them. Are you not of more value than they?" (Matt. 6:26). Jesus doesn't say birds aren't valuable. Animals are valuable because they reflect God's creation. Here Jesus is giving a "how much more" example. Animals matter, but they're not created in God's image, so humans are more valuable than animals (Gen. 1:27). The birds serve as a visual representation of God's provision. If God provides for the birds, who are not created in God's image, will he not also provide for you, a being who is?

Now a practical reason: "And which of you by being anxious can add a single hour to his span of life?" (Matt. 6:27). One person put it this way: "Worry never solved a problem, never dried a tear, never lifted a burden, never removed an obstacle. It never made bad things good or good things better." Worry cannot add a single year, month,

37

day, or even hour to your life. It may actually shorten your life. Worry is deceptive. It gives you a sense of control, but that control is illusory. It doesn't help you. It doesn't help others. It doesn't help your circumstances. It only destroys contentment. So stop worrying.

"Consider." I love that Jesus uses this word. He's encouraging his audience to think deeply. Jesus encourages faith through contemplation. How can you fight against worry? By thinking deeply on God's fatherly care.

Now to flowers, grass and clothing: "And why are you anxious about clothing? Consider the lilies of the field, how they grow: they neither toil nor spin, yet I tell you, even Solomon in all his glory was not arrayed like one of these. But if God so clothes the grass of the field, which today is alive and tomorrow is thrown into the oven, will he not much more clothe you, O you of little faith?" (Matt. 6:28-30). Flowers and grass are common Old Testament metaphors to depict the shortness and fragility of life. Flowers might be beautiful, but they don't last long. Grass might be useful, but eventually it will be cut. Jesus takes care of flowers and grass even though they don't last long. That doesn't seem productive. And that's exactly the point. If God's care extends to the fleeting grass and flowers, how much more will his care extend to you, an eternal being created in his image?

"O you of little faith."

The remedy for worry is faith.

He continues, "But seek first the kingdom of God and his righteousness, and all these things will be added to you" (Matt. 6:33). This is the climactic point. Instead of wasting energy on worry, which accomplishes nothing, channel your energy into God's kingdom advancement, which accomplishes eternal results. If you're in public and you temporarily lose your wallet, you'll vigorously search for it. This is the kind of urgency behind the meaning of the word "seek." To seek first the kingdom of God means to arrange your priorities in life so that it's unmistakably clear that God takes precedence over everything. Jesus says if you do, you don't need to worry, because he will take care of you. So much of your life is out of your control. But one aspect you can control is this: are you going to seek first the kingdom of God?

God promises necessary provision, but not freedom from trouble (Matt. 6:34). To varying degrees, every day brings trouble. But God doesn't want you to worry. He wants you to seek the kingdom and trust him.

5. Do I dwell on the past or future?

Remembering God's faithfulness in the past builds faith for the present and alleviates anxiety for the future. Reflecting on the good old days is good. But longing to be in a previous season reveals discontentment. It's also a surefire formula to miss what God is presently doing in your life. As the wise man writes, "Say not, 'Why were the former days better than these?' For it is not from wisdom that you ask this" (Eccles. 7:10).

God has placed you right now in this season of life with every particular circumstance—both good and bad—for a reason. In fact, hundreds of reasons. What are they? I don't know. And I don't think we're supposed to know. Charles Spurgeon says: "Remember this, had any other condition been better for you than the one in which you are, divine love would have put you there."[9] Although we won't have full access to God's plan during difficult seasons of life, it brings immeasurable comfort knowing you didn't arrive in this difficult season on accident. Instead of fixating on the past, God wants you to obey and enjoy him in the present.

On the other hand—and this is more of my struggle—dwelling on the future robs you of contentment because it prevents you from enjoying your life in the present. It's good to plan your days and weeks and even months. I have a strategic mind and I try to anticipate problems and create solutions for them before they arise. But we are not efficiency-monsters, created to carefully craft and follow a five-year vision statement without fail. We cannot see and

---

9.   Charles Haddon Spurgeon (1928), *Morning and Evening: Daily Readings*, p.1248, CCEL

predict the future because we are not God. You have no idea how life's events will unfold tomorrow, let alone five years from now. God has wired the universe to remind us we were created to depend on him.

Learn to live in the moment. This is the surprising difference that separated Michael Jordan from his peers. One of Jordan's biographers writes:

> Most people struggle to be present. People go and sit in ashrams for 20 years in India trying to be present. Do yoga, meditate, trying to get here, now. Most people live in fear because we project the past into the future. Michael's a mystic. He was never anywhere else. His gift was not that he could jump high, run fast, shoot a basketball. His gift was that he was completely present. And that was the separator. The big downfall of a lot of players who are otherwise gifted is thinking about failure. Michael didn't allow what he couldn't control to get inside his head. He would say, "Why would I think about missing a shot I haven't taken yet?"[10]

You don't have to buy everything this writer says to appreciate the importance of learning to live in the moment. As far as I know, Jordan isn't a Christian, and yet he was able to live in the moment better than most Christians I know, despite carrying an enormous amount of stress and pressure. How often do we miss the blessings of God in the present because we are too focused on the future?

A Contentment Prayer

Now that you have a better understanding of where you struggle with discontentment, I suggest you pause and pray. God uses prayer to change you. The model prayer below is not meant to replace the Lord's prayer or your personal praying time or praying with others. It's a prayer that encourages confession and it's best to confess sin as soon as we are made aware of it.

"O Lord God, I have sinned against you in word, attitude, and deed. I often neglect to give you thanks for the many blessings in my life. Help me to change. Grant me the desire for holiness, and may

---

10.   https://atthehelm.ca/the-cost-of-believing-what-you-think-2/

the things of this world grow less appealing to me. O Lord, let not the sinful desires of my heart continue to reign. Allow me to be content with your provision. Please forgive me for the sin of discontent and for the many ways in which I grumble and complain. Forgive me for looking to earthly possessions to give me what you alone can provide. Please grant me supernatural contentment. I ask for peace and tranquility through the ups and downs of life. May my life be characterized by continual thanksgiving and joy. And may I seek to glorify you in all I do. Amen."

Chapter 3
The Secret

"The secret is Christ in me, not me in a different set of circumstances."
— Elisabeth Elliot

The movie *Chariots of Fire* is a British sports drama that documents two athletes, Eric Liddell and Harold Abrahams, in the 1924 Olympics. Abrahams is Jewish. He is also utterly desperate for an Olympic medal. His whole life and identity are wrapped up in achieving success through running. He is noticeably unsettled and anxious throughout the movie. At one point, Abrahams was asked by a romantic partner if he loves running. He doesn't say "yes." Instead, he says he's an addict. Running is a compulsion. It's a weapon, he says, against being Jewish. He appears to run competitively to fight feelings of shame, and seeks significance through achievement.

There's a scene in the movie that reveals the secret to joy and calm amidst pressure. And that secret is contentment. While getting a massage in preparation for his race, Abrahams speaks to his friend Aubrey and says:

> You, Aubrey, are my most complete man. You're brave, compassionate, kind: a content man. That is your secret, contentment; I am twenty-four and I've never known it. I'm forever in pursuit and I don't even know what I am chasing.
>
> And now in one hour's time, I will be out there again. I will raise my eyes and look down that corridor; four feet wide, with ten lonely seconds to justify my existence. But will I?

Prison Life

I'm a sucker for a good documentary—especially one about something dangerous like a gang or life behind bars. Once I watched

43

a prison documentary about prison life in a Third World country. In this particular documentary, I was blown away by how comfortable life was for these prison inmates. They worked jobs. They had easy access to food, clothing and shelter. They went outside and enjoyed the sunlight and sports. They were allowed regular social interaction with other inmates. But this wasn't the surprising part.

Here's what surprised me most. If you're a married man in this particular prison, your wife is allowed to visit and spend the night with you. And it's not like you get a room to yourselves. Oh no, there's another inmate on the bottom bunk. No wonder the crime rates aren't getting better. The inmates don't have to get their act together if life behind bars is only slightly worse than normal life.

As you might assume, the Apostle Paul wrote the book of Philippians in a Roman prison under a different set of circumstances. After becoming greatly annoyed with a slave girl, Paul casts a demon out of her. Casting out this demon angered her owners who played a role in getting Paul locked up. Paul was first beaten with rods (Acts 16:22), and then struck with "many blows" (Acts 16:23) before being sent to prison.

Roman prisons were harsh. It was customary for those entering a Roman prison to be stripped naked, beaten and humiliated before having their feet chained and then being tossed in a cell. Inmates were often deprived of basic necessities. They often suffered abandonment from family and friends because of the social stigma of imprisonment. There was little comfort, medical care, food, or desire to release inmates in a reasonable time frame. Prisoners lived in almost complete darkness. All of this Paul endured despite not doing any wrong.[1]

You might expect Paul to be bitter under such circumstances. But he wasn't. Silas and he were "praying and singing hymns to God" (Acts 16:25). Instead of complaining about his unjust treatment, Paul

---

1. Andrew M. Davis, *The Power of Christian Contentment: Finding Deeper, Richer Christ-Centered Joy* (Ada: Baker Books, 2019), 22-23.

views his time in prison as an opportunity for gospel advancement (Phil. 1:12). Instead of grumbling and giving in to anxiety, Paul commands the Philippians against grumbling (Phil. 2:14) and anxiety (Phil. 4:6). Typically, prison inmates desire visitation to lift their spirits. But Paul writes to lift the Philippians in *their* spirits. You can feel Paul's joy and contentment throughout the letter. Joy is one of the letter's main themes. True Christian joy is not dependent on personal circumstances.

In the last chapter of Philippians, the Apostle Paul writes the most significant statement on Christian contentment in the Bible:[2]

> I rejoiced in the Lord greatly that now at length you have revived your concern for me. You were indeed concerned for me, but you had no opportunity. Not that I am speaking of being in need, for I have learned in whatever situation I am to be content. I know how to be brought low, and I know how to abound. In any and every circumstance, I have learned the secret of facing plenty and hunger, abundance and need. I can do all things through him who strengthens me (Phil. 4:10-13).[3]

The Secret

Paul expresses thanks for the gifts received through Epaphroditus (Phil. 4:18), sent by the only church supporting Paul during this prison sentence (Phil. 4:15). Verse 10 is a transitional sentence: "I rejoiced in the Lord greatly that now at length you have revived your concern for me." It could be misread to imply Paul was neglected by the Philippians for a time, but Paul shows understanding: "You were indeed concerned for me, but you had no opportunity." The Philippians wanted to support Paul, but there was not yet an opportunity. But now in God's timing, Epaphroditus was available to send the gifts.

Curiously, Paul never directly thanks the Philippians for their gifts, and he doesn't rejoice in the gifts themselves. "I rejoiced in the Lord greatly," Paul says. These six words are crucial for

2. Andrew M. Davis, *The Power of Christian Contentment*, 20.
3. This chapter is not an academic explanation of Philippians 4:10-13, but rather brief devotional meditations with a specific emphasis on contentment.

understanding Christian contentment. This is the only use of "greatly" in the New Testament and the only place in Paul's letters where he explicitly mentions his own encounter with joy.[4] A similar kind of joy is mentioned when the wise men in Matthew's Gospel saw the star and "rejoiced exceedingly with great joy" (Matt. 2:10).

What does rejoicing mean? It's not a never-ending, happy-clappy feeling. To put it simply, rejoicing means to make your soul glad in God. George Müller famously said the first and most important thing he must do every morning is "have my soul happy in the Lord." Rejoicing in the Lord is an intentional spiritual decision. Usually, rejoicing in the Lord occurs through the means of grace, spiritual disciplines, meditating on the gospel, reflecting on God's faithfulness, or expressing thanksgiving. Regardless of the means you utilize, you must take the initiative.

Rejoicing in the Lord is independent of circumstances. Even when your circumstances feel unbearable, rejoicing is still possible because the basis for rejoicing is God's character, not your circumstances. After King David was greatly distressed because he thought he might be stoned to death for family captivity, he "strengthened himself in the Lord his God" (1 Sam. 30:6). Or consider the way J.I. Packer says it: "Even when we cannot see the why and the wherefore of God's dealings, we know that there is love in and behind them, and so we can rejoice always, even when, humanly speaking, things are going wrong."[5]

Is it wrong to get excited about people or possessions? No. But people and possessions cannot be the source of your joy because they're finite and perishing. If your circumstances regularly alter your joy, then too much of your joy is dependent on your circumstances. God and God alone can be trusted as the basis for rejoicing. The Lord is a rock who never changes, can never be shaken, and can be trusted and rejoiced in now and for all eternity. Learning to rejoice in the Lord is a prerequisite for Christian contentment.

4. Gerald F. Hawthrone, *Word Biblical Commentary: Volume 43 Philippians, first edition* (Waco: Word Books, 1983), 196.
5. J.I. Packer, *Knowing God* (Westmont: IVP, 1993), 122.

Learning Contentment

In verse 11, Paul writes more specifically about contentment: "Not that I am speaking of being in need, for I have learned in whatever situation I am to be content."

Paul says he *learned* contentment. Isn't it encouraging to know that the great Apostle Paul had to learn contentment? Paul was brilliant, spoke several languages, was a "Hebrew of Hebrews," a former high-profile Pharisee who studied under the main instructor (Acts 22:3), a master in the law, one who was zealous for the church, and a naturally intelligent and a highly accomplished Roman citizen who enjoyed privileges because of his citizenship. And yet, even Paul had to learn contentment. It didn't come naturally for him. It won't come naturally for you.

Puritan Thomas Watson observes that Paul doesn't say "I have heard" but "I have learned." Many Christians have an idea of contentment, but have not experienced its effects. Mentally agreeing that contentment is valuable is far different than enjoying inner peace and joy during a difficult trial. And notice, Paul speaks about contentment in first person: "*I* have learned." You have to learn contentment for yourself.

"Learned" is used twice (Phil. 4:11, 12). Not only is the use of repetition a reminder to the reader that contentment must be learned, but the meanings of the words differ. The term for "learned" in verse 11 is the kind of learning you normally think of—acquiring knowledge or skill through instruction or experience. The verb "learned" in verse 12, however, comes from the word "mystery"— a commonly used word in Paul's day. "Mystery" was used in the Greek mystery religions of Paul's era. It means "to be initiated," as in initiated into various rituals of other religions or secret societies. Here, Paul is flipping the meaning and uses the word "mystery" (a.k.a. "learned") in verse 12 to distinguish between how Christians and unbelievers learn contentment.[6] What's the difference? Paul explains. But not yet.

Biblical Contentment

The word "content" in this famous passage comes from two words which, when put together, means "self-sufficient." As we have already seen, that's the biblical idea of contentment. "Self-sufficient" as the biblical definition of contentment in the Bible may surprise you since growing as a Christian means learning *dependence* on God. But Paul is not advocating self-dependence. Once again, Paul uses language from the common worldviews of his time to connect with his readers. Here, the worldview Paul is confronting is stoicism. The goal of stoicism was "that man should be sufficient unto himself for all things, and able, by the power of his own will, to resist the force of circumstance."[7] As discussed in chapter one, Stoics sought to live without need, undeterred by circumstances. Seeking self-sufficiency through internal strength was, and remains, its aim. Paul is Christianizing the stoic understanding of contentment.[8] Paul has learned contentment, but not like the stoics. Gordon Fee rightly says: ". . . he [Paul] turns 'self-sufficiency' into 'contentment' because of his 'Christ-sufficiency.'"[9]

Contentment in Suffering

"I know how to be brought low, and I know how to abound," Paul continues (4:12). Paul was content in "whatever situation," including suffering. 2 Corinthians 11:23-28 lists some of Paul's sufferings:

> Are they servants of Christ? I am a better one—I am talking like a madman—with far greater labors, far more imprisonments, with countless beatings, and often near death. Five times I received at the hands of the Jews the forty lashes less one. Three times

---

6. William B. Barcley, *The Secret of Contentment* (Phillipsburg: P&R Publishing, 2010), 25.
7. Gerald F. Hawthrone, *Word Biblical Commentary: Volume 43 Philippians, first edition*, 198.
8. Gordon Fee, *Paul's Letter to the Philippians* (Grand Rapids: Eerdmans, 1995), 425.
9. Ibid, 434.

I was beaten with rods. Once I was stoned. Three times I was shipwrecked; a night and a day I was adrift at sea; on frequent journeys, in danger from rivers, danger from robbers, danger from my own people, danger from Gentiles, danger in the city, danger in the wilderness, danger at sea, danger from false brothers; in toil and hardship, through many a sleepless night, in hunger and thirst, often without food, in cold and exposure. And, apart from other things, there is the daily pressure on me of my anxiety for all the churches (2 Cor. 11:23-28).

It's difficult to comprehend this list (and there's more Paul could have added). Imagine almost being beaten to death several times, without food, and in danger from those who could kill you. A friend of mine recently shared that he is afraid of the ocean. I told him the ocean is a good thing to be afraid of. I live a mile from the Atlantic Ocean and have seen firsthand the danger of rip currents and crashing waves and windy waters. Just recently where I live, a nineteen-year-old refugee drowned by trying to save a family in a rip current. Paul was "adrift at sea" and battled against "danger from rivers." Chilling words. But it was in these moments Paul learned contentment. Often, God teaches contentment through suffering.

I went to a professional golf tournament with a friend of mine. Like the thousands of others in attendance, I was amazed at how effortless the golfers made it look. Anyone who tries golf knows at first it's extremely hard. Golf is one of the few sports that can make a naturally good athlete look like a fool. I wish I could get the spotlight in front of thousands of people, hit a little white ball into a hole, and gain the accolades that accompany golf success. But I'm not willing to suffer and sacrifice thousands of hours in private to become a good golfer.

We desire contentment, but only like a cure-all pill: take this pill, and in twenty minutes, you'll feel better. But contentment doesn't work instantly. Contentment derives from long and painful seasons of pain, sorrow and discomfort.

When suffering, we desire relief. That's normal. But when life isn't going well, we should ask, "What might God be trying to teach me in this trial?" We can't always know for sure, but surely God is teaching you to be content.

A pastor once used a metaphor to describe God like a wise and perfect doctor and his people as the sick patients. We are prone to love earthly blessings more than God. And so God, being the great physician that he is, sends us distasteful trials, hardships that are hard to swallow, and cuts us open before providing the surgical healing. Suffering is an extremely painful yet necessary process in learning contentment. When going through trials, you can pray for a new set of circumstances, but you should also pray for contentment in your circumstances.

Contentment in Success

Jeremiah Burroughs ends his classic work on contentment with a quick thought on Paul's words, "I have learned to abound." Writes Burroughs, "That does not so nearly concern us at this time, because the times are afflictive times . . . there are few who have such an abundance that they need to be much taught in that lesson."[10] Oh, how the times have changed. Christians in the Western world today are abounding more than ever, but the abundance hasn't led to happiness. I've never met a person who desired to learn contentment because their life was going well. But it's essential to learn contentment when abounding.

It sounds like a contradiction, but contentment is harder when abounding than when suffering. When suffering, we run to God. We're more open to pray, share our burdens, and seek help. But during times of prosperity, we become spiritually lethargic. We stop feeling dependent on God and might even feel superior to others who are suffering. Paul knows how to "abound" and face abundance (v. 12). Ordinarily, abundance is not something we think we need to face. We don't see it as a challenge. But prosperity is a test. Most Christians don't have the character to handle an unusual amount of success without it hurting their character in some way.

---

10.   Burroughs, *Rare Jewel*, 228.

When the money is high, the health is good, and all seems well with your world, you must continue to rejoice in the Lord and learn contentment.

I know of no better way to practice contentment in seasons of success than to understand all that you have comes from the Lord, and one day you will give an account to him for how you stewarded all that was entrusted to you. Consider, for example, the Israelites before entering the Promised Land. The Lord provides warnings to guard their hearts, lest they think the good food and the nice houses and money and other forms of prosperity they enjoy are due to *their* power. (Deut. 8:11-20). The Lord warns they will perish if they forget the Lord and his commands.

Prosperity doesn't automatically bring contentment. Some of the most miserable people in the world are rich and famous secular people. A successful entrepreneur may tell you that the success of his business only increased his anxiety. Many single Christians who idolize marriage are jarred when they discover marriage cannot complete them. Single Christians may think marriage will solve their problems, but Paul says marriage will increase your problems (1 Cor. 7:28). Most of us underestimate how much a great deal of success in our profession will hurt us. When the Lord sends abundance, may we say with the Psalmist: "As for me, I said in my prosperity, 'I shall never be moved'" (Ps. 30:6).

The Strength of Jesus

Paul builds his case. He starts with the Philippians' acknowledgment of his well-being (v.10), admits his lack of need because of his supply of contentment (v.11), and shares the circumstances that taught him contentment (v.12). But Paul hasn't told us exactly how he experienced contentment—until now: "I can do all things through him who strengthens me" (Phil. 4:13).

Philippians 4:13 is one of the most popular and misapplied Bible verses in all of Scripture. In order to get a better understanding of how some regard these famous words, I typed "Philippians 4:13" into the Twitter search bar, something I don't necessarily recommend.

Athletic and personal achievements dominated the search. I saw pictures of people hitting baseballs, dunking basketballs, and walking across stages to receive diplomas. All good accomplishments. But they misrepresent the specific meaning of Paul's words.

Like all Bible verses, this verse must be understood in its context. And the specific context of Paul's comments in Philippians 4:13 relates to contentment through good times and bad. When Paul says he can do "all things through him who strengthens me," he's not saying he can *accomplish* anything, but *endure* anything. Think endurance, not accomplishments. And, of course, Jesus is the one who strengthens Paul. The word "strengthens" is a present participle—in other words, this is not a one-time filling of strength but a continual, ongoing filling of strength from Jesus. The supernatural strength that Jesus supplies is the way to be content in all circumstances. That's the secret to contentment.

This is what separates a Christian perspective on contentment from a secular view. In the Christian faith, true contentment is possible because Christ empowers his people by divine enablement, providing them supernatural strength to endure anything. It takes Christ's power to experience contentment. We often overestimate our own power and underestimate how much we need God's power to get through life.

Sometimes I read stories about Christians who endure a tremendous amount of hardship with joy. These people in other countries are being tortured for their beliefs and somehow they manage to get through with unwavering faith. I think to myself, "How in the world are they able to endure when they are being harassed by enemies?" Because God supernaturally provides his people strength to endure trials.

God gives you what you need when you need it. But he doesn't give you strength today to handle next week's issues. No, he gives you strength today to handle today's issues and that's it. Today, you must come to him. Tomorrow, you must do the same. God operates this way because he wants you to learn dependence on him. He knows that if he gives you what you need today for the next few months, eventually you'll wander from the fold, so to speak, and strain your fellowship with him. He loves you too much to allow you to live independently. Deriving strength from Jesus is like sleep, something you need daily, not like filling your car with gas, something you do every couple of weeks. Daily, even hourly, we need to be strengthened by the supernatural power of Christ. Through ups and downs, highs and lows, suffering and success. No matter what good or bad God sends your way, you can endure with contentment because of supernatural strength.

The story is told of a dad who asked his young boy to lift a heavy object. The task was clearly beyond the strength of the young boy, but his father asked him anyway. The young boy tried, and tried, and tried, but he just could not do it. "Try again," the father said. Still, no success. "Son," the father said, "you're still not accessing all of your strength." The boy tried again but failed. "Son, you're still not using all your strength." Finally, the young boy blurted out, "Oh, daddy, daddy; I'm trying as hard as I can as I use all my strength." The father replied, "No you're not, son. You haven't asked me for help."[11]

How often do you go through life trying to endure difficulties on your own when you have an all-powerful God who is ready to help?

Habakkuk Encounters Contentment

Contentment is attainable but not automatic. How it works is a bit mysterious. For example, what about when you earnestly pray for strength and feel weaker after praying? Or what about when you feel zero satisfaction after expressing gratitude? In these moments, we must particularly trust God's character. By faith, we have to trust that, while we are obeying God's word, he is working contentment in us even when we feel like he isn't. The promises of Scripture surpasses our feelings and subjective assessments.

Habakkuk learned the secret of contentment. He had to. The theme of the book bearing his name is trusting and waiting on God.

---

11.   Robert D. Jones, *Contentment: Joy That Lasts* (Phillipsburg: P&R, 2019), 23.

In the beginning of the book, Habakkuk complains to God about perceived injustices. Habakkuk laments because God doesn't seem to be answering Habakkuk's specific prayer requests. He thinks God is aloof amidst the wickedness in society. But God does answer his prayers and punish the wicked, just not on Habakkuk's timetable. After wrestling with God, Habakkuk is, by the end of the book, a changed man. He begins to understand that God works in ways beyond his comprehension. He's learned to rejoice in the Lord. He's learned to trust the goodness of God despite unanswered questions:

> Though the fig tree should not blossom,
> nor fruit be on the vines,
> the produce of the olive fail
> and the fields yield no food,
> the flock be cut off from the fold
> and there be no herd in the stalls,
> yet I will rejoice in the Lord;
> I will take joy in the God of my salvation.
> God, the Lord, is my strength;
> he makes my feet like the deer's;
> he makes me tread on my high places (Hab. 3:17-19).

Future provision is no guarantee (v. 17). Like Paul, Habakkuk and his people may face hunger. He's living with the severe uncertainty about not having the basic necessities of life. But also, like Paul, Habakkuk decides to "rejoice in the Lord" (v. 18). He chooses to "take joy in the God of my salvation" (v. 18b). The Lord is his strength. In turn, the Lord "makes my feet like the deer's; and he makes me tread on my high places" (v. 19). This is, of course, metaphorical language to describe the contentment Habakkuk experiences in light of his rejoicing in the Lord and the strength the Lord provides. Habakkuk's encounter with God reinforces the lesson that God's people have been learning for thousands of years: true Christian contentment is possible regardless of circumstances.

Part 2:

Applying Contentment

Chapter 4
Money and Possessions

"I have heard of some good old woman in a cottage, who had nothing but a piece of bread and a little water. Lifting up her hands, she said as a blessing, 'What! All this, and Christ too?' — Charles Spurgeon

On Christmas Eve 2002, an ordinary fifty-five-year-old construction worker from West Virginia, Andrew Jackson Whittaker Jr., who goes by "Jack," stopped at a supermarket for a routine gas and sandwich visit. The national Powerball lottery was generating nationwide attention, reaching a whopping $314.9 million. At the time, it was the largest jackpot in American history. Purchasing a lottery ticket was abnormal behavior for Whittaker, but he decided on a whim to purchase over $100 worth of tickets. Whittaker didn't need the money. He was already a millionaire, raking in $17 million a year from construction work.

The day after Christmas, Whittaker was verified as the sole winner of the lottery. "I'm very blessed," he told reporters. He continued: "I've been blessed my whole life. It's really going to excite my daughter and granddaughter. They're going to be spending the money." He also talked about taking care of his family and expanding his business. He chose to receive the money by cash immediately, instead of annually and gradually through direct deposit. After taxes, Whittaker received $113.4 million. As a member of the Church of God, Whittaker desired to give away 10 percent of his money before spending it, so his first three checks were written to pastors. "I just want to thank God," Whittaker said, "for letting the machine pick the right numbers."

Overnight, Whittaker became a national celebrity and was flown to New York on a private jet within twenty-four hours after winning the lottery to be on national television so millions could learn his plans for the money. And being true to his word, Whittaker gave money away to his family—buying four cars and giving $2,000 a week to his granddaughter, Brandi Bragg. When asked if four cars were too much for a teenager, Whittaker replied, "She can only drive one at a time." Bragg's money attracted a new boyfriend, a young man named Jesse. Together, Jesse and Brandi developed a drug addiction, and Jesse overdosed and died shortly after they began dating. Drugs also destroyed Brandi, who lost interest in anything besides getting high. She, too, soon died and her body was found in a plastic bag on the property of a male friend less than two years later. No one was charged for her death.

Problems multiplied for Whittaker who infamously carried his money in a suitcase. "Because I can," Whittaker would say, when asked why he carried his money this way. Whittaker struggled with alcohol, gambling, got divorced, and incurred multiple DUIs. His house and cars were repeatedly robbed. He even was robbed in person multiple times, once for over $500,000 at a strip club. His ex said that she wished he had torn the ticket in half. He said he wished he had done the same. He died in the summer of 2020 from "natural causes."[1]

The Blessing and Seduction of Wealth

Wealth is a blessing. It's possible to be rich and honor God. Lydia was a successful businesswoman who stewarded her possessions by serving Paul and others (Acts 16:14). King David was rich and famous and was at one time labeled "a man after God's own heart" (1 Sam. 13:14). Joseph of Arimathea, the man who wrapped Jesus' body in a clean linen shroud, was described as "a rich man" but also as "a disciple of Jesus" (Matt. 27:57). Job was also wealthy and was labeled by God as "blameless," "upright," and unmatched in integrity across all the earth (Job 1:8). Throughout Scripture we see men and women of God

---

1. John Raby, "From Powerball winner to scandal: Jack Whittaker dies at 72," *AP News*, June 2020, https://apnews.com/article/wv-state-wire-lifestyle-ap-top-news-us-news-obituaries-97c2aae5522a9d39ef5e5bbfa2d364d0

who were rich and honor him (at least for a season), and today there are thousands of Christians who effectively steward their wealth to advance God's kingdom causes.

And yet, let me hasten to say that wealth provides unique temptations to sin—and not just having wealth, but even *desiring* wealth too much—can cause a spiritual shipwreck. Why? Because wealth is seductive. It can trap and seduce you into self-worship (sometimes unknowingly) and turn your heart away from God. Often, material prosperity leads to spiritual complacency. Ross Douthat, in his provocative book *Bad Religion: How We Became a Nation of Heretics,* considers explosive growth in material prosperity in the twenty-first century and the "prosperity gospel" preachers who advocate this lifestyle, as a reason for Christendom's downfall in America.[2] Why need God when provision is acquired so easily? Or why pursue spiritual satisfaction in God when you already find satisfaction from wealth, comfort and material possessions? Material prosperity is one of the reasons why Christianity is flourishing in many less developed nations but struggling in many of the prosperous ones.

Prosperity theology says true Christians are rich; poverty theology says true Christians are poor. Both are wrong. The wise man desires "neither poverty nor riches" (Prov. 30:8). Poverty and affluence both create specific temptations to sin. Rich or poor, the issue for Christians is not whether you have wealth, but your heart's desire toward it and how you are stewarding it.[3]

Curiously, most of the teachings in the Bible about contentment address wealth. Let's look at some of those passages.

---

2. Admittedly, Douthat spends most of the chapter (ch. 6, "Pray and Grow Rich") focusing on prosperity gospel preachers in particular, but the widespread prosperity in the twenty-first century makes it easier for prosperity preachers to have a voice. The sheer volume of adherents to their false message has led to confusion about what it means to be a Christian. See Ross Douthat, *Bad Religion: How We Became a Nation of Heretics* (New York, Free Press, 2012).

3. John Frame, *The Doctrine of the Christian Life* (Phillipsburg: P&R Publishing, 2008), 810.

Contentment in Hebrews

The author of Hebrews writes:

"Keep your life free from love of money, and be content with what you have, for he has said, 'I will never leave you nor forsake you.' So we can confidently say, 'The Lord is my helper; I will not fear; what can man do to me?'" (Heb. 13:5-6).

Hebrews is written by an unnamed author to a group of God's people who are being persecuted for their faith. So far they've handled the persecution well: ". . . you joyfully accepted the plundering of your property, since you knew that you yourselves had a better position and an abiding one" (Heb. 10:34). They were persecuted once and they could be persecuted again. When you live with reality that your life may be in danger, it's tempting to succumb to anxiety and cling to wealth for a sense of security. But the writer of Hebrews promotes a different way; he provides assurance with the promises of God.

The writer of Hebrews doesn't say to keep your life free from money, but from the love of money. Paul also says, "For the *love of money* is a root of all kinds of evils" (1 Tim. 6:10). Loving money is prohibited. This principle aligns with the teachings of Jesus who says, "You cannot serve God and money" (Matt. 6:24). In Scripture, the biblical authors promote a Creator–creation distinction to show how to properly worship God. God is the Creator, and everything else (e.g. money, people, food, and so on) is creation. We are free to enjoy creation, but not worship it. We must worship God and God alone. The essence of idolatry is when the Creator–creation order is reversed.

Having abundant wealth and seeking more for the right reasons is allowable. John Wesley, for example, encouraged believers to make, give and save as much money as possible. Some Christians are rich because they have received a large inheritance, come from a rich family, or providentially find themselves wealthy through God's blessing in their career. Believers in this position should shake off any feelings of false guilt and seek to steward their resources properly. According to Hebrews 13:5, to gauge faithfulness with your money, the proper question is not, "Are you rich?" but "Are you keeping your life free from the love of money?"

What's the problem with loving money? Loving money will distract you from worshiping God correctly. It will also make you anxious, restless and self-absorbed. If the love of money is a root of all kinds of evil, then selfishness is a root of the love of money. People who love money tend to be extremely self-centered. Loving money not only resembles an attitude of the Pharisees who were "lovers of money" (Luke 16:14), but the love of money disqualifies a person from being a pastor (1 Tim. 3:3). The love of money cannot and will not make you happy, for, "He who loves money will not be satisfied with money, nor he who loves wealth with his income" (Eccles. 5:10). The love of money often ends in walking away from God. It's a lose (sin against God), lose (sin against neighbor), lose (incurs misery).

Contentment is Commanded

"Be content with what you have," says the writer of Hebrews, implying that you don't need anything in addition to what you currently own in order to experience contentment. "Be content" is a command, as when Jesus says "do not worry" (Matt. 6:34) and when Paul says "flee from sexual immorality" (1 Cor. 6:18). Words like these in Scripture are not merely good advice, practical "how-to's," or take it or leave it thoughts. No, these are commands from God himself. And notice the link. The words, "Keep your life free from the love of money" and "be content with what you have" are connected: the way you avoid the love of money is through contentment; the way you obtain contentment is by not loving money.

There are many Bible passages that join contentment to wealth. When John the Baptist, for example, was preaching forgiveness and repentance, some listening asked how they should respond to John's teachings. He replied, "Do not extort money from anyone by threats or false accusation, and be content with your wages" (Luke 3:14). When the Apostle Paul wanted to thank the Philippians indirectly for their provision, he ensured his lack of need by saying, "Not that I am speaking of being in need, for I have learned in whatever situation I am to be content" (Phil. 4:11). Before warning his readers that the love of money is a root of all kinds of evil, Paul says "godliness with contentment is great gain" (1 Tim. 6:6) and adds that having food and clothing is sufficient grounds for contentment (1 Tim. 6:8). The frustratingly simple yet altogether liberating cure for the love of money is contentment.

Contentment is commanded. But as is often the case in Scripture, this command coexists with a promise.

God Will Never Leave You

Hebrews has many warnings about not leaving Christ (Heb. 5-7). But the author also assures his readers that Christ won't leave them: "I will never leave you nor forsake you" (Heb. 13:5b). Five negatives are used in the Greek grammar of this verse. It's as if the writer is saying, "I will never, never, never, never, never leave or forsake you." Typically, we encourage people to avoid using the word "never." "Never say 'never,'" we say. If we say we're never going to do something and then we commit that particular action, we undermine our credibility. Weeks before my seminary graduation, a friend asked if I was ever going to visit our seminary's library again, to which I vouched I never would, only to return a few months after graduating.

But God is free to use words like "never" in relation to his actions because his promises always come true. The reason why you shouldn't love money and should be content with what you have is because God will never leave or forsake you. The idea that God will never leave you also implies he will provide for you. So the logic is: (1) Don't love money; (2) Be Content; (3) God will never leave you. Numbers one and two are possible because number three is true. The more the reality of God's fatherly care penetrates the deep recesses of your soul, the less likely you'll love money and the more contentment will be attainable.

The quotation "I will never leave or forsake you" is found often in the Old Testament. When God met Jacob in a dream to remind him that the promises given to Abraham would be established through Jacob, he says, "Behold, I am with you and will keep you wherever you go . . . For I will not leave you until I have done what I have promised you" (Gen. 28:15). When Joshua was charged with the daunting task of leading the Israelites into the Promised Land, the Lord reminds him, "No man shall be able to stand before you all the days of your life. Just as I was with Moses, so I will be with you. I will not leave you or forsake you" (Josh. 1:5). When David publicly charged Solomon to build a temple, he said, ". . . Do not be afraid and do not be dismayed, for the Lord God, even my God, is with you. He will not leave you or forsake you, until all the work for the service of the house of the Lord is finished" (1 Chron. 28:20). What is true for these Old Testament figures is also true for you. As you obey the Lord, the Lord promises that he will be with you every step of the way.

I picked up my toddler from in-home daycare one day, only to find him crying. I don't like seeing him cry and when he does I almost always assume the sitter did something wrong, but experience tells me to ask questions before making judgments. So I asked the sitter why my son was crying. The babysitter told me that when my son is the last child picked up, he starts crying, presumably because he wonders if daddy is going to pick him up or not. My heart ached that moment as my sweet boy ran into my arms. Before getting into the car to go home, I placed my sixteen-month-old on the back of my car and said, with the most loving voice I could muster, "Son, listen." I continued: "I will never, ever forget to pick you up—*ever*. Daddy will always be here for you." The next day, I picked him up 30 minutes earlier than normal to ensure he would be the first kid picked up.

You must believe God cares for and will never abandon you. He doesn't promise a successful career, a long life or good health, but he does promise to be with you always, a promise which is far better than any material blessing.

The Lord is My Helper

"So we can confidently say," says the author of Hebrews, as he ends this section on contentment (13:6), that "The Lord is my helper; I will not fear." Confidently means "to have certainty in a matter, be confident, be courageous."[4] Certainty. Confidence. Courage. In what? This quotation appears in Psalm 118:6 where the psalmist writes, "The Lord is on my side; I will not fear. What can man do to me?" This Psalm is a joyful song of thanksgiving, part of which describes a personal rescue from a distressing situation. The psalmist's taste of the Lord's help in the past removes anxiety for potentially distressing future scenarios. He even asks: "What can man do to me?" Well, a man can assault him for his faith. Or he can ruin his reputation. He can, most specifically for this context, steal his wealth. Persecution may cause poverty which was a real threat for the intended audience of the letter of Hebrews and for many Christians today. But the question is not meant to be answered; it's rhetorical. Actually, it's more of a boast than a question. The writer is boasting in the Lord. Despite any worse case scenario imaginable for the psalmist or the intended recipients of the letter of Hebrews, the Lord is their helper, so there's no reason to fear.

How often do you ponder the faithfulness of God in your life? Like the Israelites who were dramatically rescued from slavery but wondered if God would provide them with something to eat, we experience God's provision, quickly thank him (or not), and then arrest our attention on escaping the next trial. Personal remembrance of God's faithfulness is one of the most important spiritual disciplines in the Christian life. This discipline builds faith in God's character for your present circumstances and alleviates fear for the future.

---

4. BDAG, p. 444.

Contentment and Godliness

Paul says:

"But godliness with contentment is great gain, for we brought nothing into the world, and we cannot take anything out of the world. But if we have food and clothing, with these we will be content" (1 Tim. 6:6-8).

Godliness is a major theme in Paul's letters to Timothy. He writes in part to give Timothy instructions on how to deal with false teachers in the church. These heretics, "depraved in mind" and "deprived of the truth," believed that "godliness is a means of gain" (1 Tim. 6:5). They taught that growth in godliness is evidenced by growth in financial riches. This error is corrected by Paul who says: "But godliness with contentment is great gain" (1 Tim. 6:6). Paul also speaks of gain— in fact, *great* gain—but not as the false teachers do. Unlike the false teachers, Paul teaches that growing in godliness, coupled with contentment, is proof of gain.

Paul doesn't say financial gain is wrong, just that it's not a sign of godliness. He puts wealth in its place. He discusses personal exercise in a similar way earlier in his letter when he says that "bodily training is of some value" (1 Tim. 4:8). Exercise, dieting and taking vitamins are good ways to steward your body. I feel much better about life when I exercise regularly and eat healthy foods. Healthy habits help for this life, but "godliness is of value in every way, as it holds promise for the present life and also for the life to come" (1 Tim. 4:8). All the essential oils in the world cannot prevent death. Eventually, all Christians will receive perfect, transformed bodies (Phil. 3:21), but the upsides of diligent health habits cease at death. While bodily training is helpful for this life only, godliness is essential for this life and for the life to come. For this life, growth in godliness gives you the pleasure of pleasing Christ as you become more like him. For the next, godliness now means more influence and treasures in heaven (2 Cor. 5:10). From an opportunity cost perspective, godliness is more valuable than exercise.

Similarly, godliness is more valuable than money. Why? Paul's simple argument: "for we brought nothing into the world, and we cannot take anything out of the world" (1 Tim. 6:7). It's hard to find more practical advice in all of Scripture. Randy Alcorn provides a helpful image when he reminds us that, "You'll never see a hearse pulling a U-Haul."[5] His point, and Paul's point too, is you can't take any of your amassed wealth into eternity, so to have an unnecessary amount of it is foolish. Job voices something akin to Paul's counsel when, after news of personal tragedies reaches his ears, he remarkably falls to the ground and says: "Naked I came from my mother's womb, and naked shall I return" (Job 1:21a).

Birth and death provide a unique opportunity to evaluate what matters most. In one sociological study, fifty people over the age of ninety-five were asked a pointed question: "If you could live your life over again, what would you do differently?" Three themes dominated the survey answers: (1) I would reflect more; (2) I would risk more; and—get this one —(3) I would do more things that would live on after I am dead.[6] I've never heard anyone on their deathbed say, "Gee. I'm sure glad I neglected my family and church to seek more wealth." Even if you've accumulated significant wealth, you still have to pass it on to the next guy and "who knows whether he will be wise or a fool?" (Eccles. 2:19).

It's time to take eternity seriously. Consider the third survey answer again: "I would do more things that would live on after I am dead." Can you perceive the deep longing of eternity God has placed in the human heart? (Eccles. 3:11). As a believer, you have an opportunity to make an eternal impact both for yourself and others. You are storing up imperishable treasure for yourself in heaven as you faithfully steward the resources God has entrusted to you

---

5. Randy Alcorn, *The Treasure Principle: Unlocking the Secret of Joyful Giving* (Colorado Springs: Multnomah, 2017), 10.

6. John Maxwell, *Leadership 101: What Every Leader Needs to Know* (New York City: HarperCollins Leadership), 38.

(Matt. 6:19-21). Jonathan Edwards, the great American theologian, once penned a list of seventy resolutions. Here's number twenty-two: "Resolved, to endeavor to obtain for myself as much happiness, in the other world, as I possibly can . . ." We are saved by God's grace alone, but our present good works done for God's glory lead to greater influence and treasures in heaven (Matt. 25:14-30). An eternal perspective is foundational if you want to handle God's money well.

The Litmus Test for Contentment

What is the litmus test for contentment? Many Western Christians think contentment means opting out of buying a second home, enjoying two vacations a year instead of four, or going out to eat twice a week instead of every day. This sort of thinking reveals just how much we struggle with the idol of consumerism. Instead of a slightly less luxurious life, the Apostle Paul has a different benchmark in mind when considering the grounds for contentment: "But if we have food and clothing, with these we will be content" (1 Tim. 6:8). One Bible scholar rightly says this powerful verse is often ignored.[7] According to Paul, if you have food and clothing—which is a way of saying the basic necessities of life—you should be content. Paul doesn't even say *how* the basic necessities of life will produce contentment; he just assumes they will. No elaboration needed. If fact, he puts it strongly: "we will be content."

Wealth is unnecessary for contentment, and neither is it necessary for personal well-being. According to one psychologist, "Research on the happiness of wealthy and poor people makes it clear that how much we have bears relatively little relationship to our well-being, beyond the point of ensuring sufficient food, shelter, and clothing to survive."[8] Sounds like Paul: "if we have food and clothing, with these we will be content."

---

7.   William D. Mounce, *Word Biblical Commentary: Pastoral Epistles* (Grand Rapids: Zondervan, 200), 343.

8.   Tim Kasser, *The High Price of Materialism* (Cambridge: MIT Press, 2002), 4.

If you think the bar for contentment is low, know that it could be lower. There are examples in the Bible, and even many Christians today don't have the basic necessities of life and, somehow, they're still content. Through the power of Scripture, for instance, Jesus remained content in the wilderness despite fasting and severe attacks from the enemy (Matt. 4:1-11). The Paul who tells Timothy to be content with food and clothing is the same Paul who learned contentment "in hunger and thirst, often without food" (2 Cor. 11:27). Some in the Hall of Faith chapter (Heb. 11) were "destitute," "afflicted," "mistreated," and even "wandering about in deserts and mountains, and in dens and in caves of the earth" (Heb. 11:37-38).

If you have the basic necessities of life, you already have what you need to experience Christian contentment.

God, Possessions and Greed

Greed is the desire to have more than what you need. Paul calls it idolatry (Col. 3:5; Eph. 5:5). When Tim Keller, former senior pastor of Redeemer Presbyterian Church in New York City, prepared a series of teachings on the Seven Deadly Sins for a men's breakfast, his wife predicted the lesson on greed would be the least attended. She was right. I forgot that greed was even on the list, probably revealing that I struggle with it in some way. I'm not alone. Why would so many men show up to hear Keller speak on lust and pride but not attend when greed is the subject? Probably because they don't think they struggle with it. Or perhaps they think greed is not affecting their lives if they do. Their assumptions are incorrect. Greed is a widespread sin struggle that is frequently overlooked. As Keller writes, "Jesus warns people far more often about greed than about sex, yet almost no one thinks they are guilty of it."[9]

Charles Spurgeon, in a way that only Charles Spurgeon could, writes about greedy people:

---

9. Tim Keller, *Counterfeit Gods*, 52-3.

It is not possible to satisfy the greedy. If God gave them one whole world to themselves they would cry for another; and if it were possible for them to possess heaven as they now are, they would feel themselves in hell, because others were in heaven too, for their greed is such that they must have everything or else they have nothing.[10]

Jesus gives the parable of the rich fool in response to a comment about dividing a family inheritance in order to show the insignificance of material possessions (Luke 12:13-21). After telling the greedy inquisitor that it's not his job to deal with family inheritance issues, Jesus says, "Watch out! Be on your guard against all kinds of greed; life does not consist in an abundance of possessions" (Luke 12:15 NIV). In this striking verse, Jesus gives the double warning of "Watch out!" and "Be on your guard" to provide emphasis on his teachings to guard your heart against greed. He's describing the offensive posture his disciples should model to fight against greed. Usually, we're on guard when we perceive something bad may happen to us or someone we love, but we don't take this posture with greed because we don't think we struggle with it or that it's not hurting us that much if we do. But greed is sneaky and insidious. It has a way of making you feel like you don't struggle with it when you actually might. This is especially true if you consider how you allocate your wealth compared to your secular friends or less mature Christians. It's possible to handle your wealth better than others and still be greedy. The faithfulness test with wealth is not if we're stewarding our resources better than our neighbor, but if we're properly stewarding our wealth according to the Bible's teachings.

So we must watch out, be on guard, as Jesus says, against greed. The story about the rich fool follows. He was a successful farmer, this rich fool, with no place left for the extra crops. Success is a blessing. But as it often does, it got the best of this farmer: "Then he said, 'This is what I'll do. I will tear down my barns and build bigger

---

10. Quoted in R. Kent Hughes, *Hebrews: An Anchor for the Soul* (Wheaton: Crossway, 2015), 449.

ones, and there I will store my surplus grain'" (Luke 12:18 NIV). Bigger ones. *My* surplus. Enough surplus to last many years, or so he thinks. To celebrate his success, the farmer decides to eat, drink and be merry, which are all good, but the problem with the fool is the false sense of security he derives from his amassed wealth. He becomes complacent; he thinks he's invincible. But on the same day he says he's going to be merry and enjoy the pleasure of eating and drinking, he dies. He did not think about his eternal soul, something far more precious than earthly treasures. The point of the parable is that material possessions provide a false sense of security, and a right relationship with God is more valuable than wealth (Matt. 16:26), and instead of self-indulgence, disciples should be rich toward God (Luke 12:21). The rich fool failed to have an eternal perspective.

What's the big deal with material possessions anyway? Why have they stolen the hearts of millions? Similar to money, the chase for more material possessions is not in the possessions itself, but in what we think possessions can give us: approval, security, status. Ultimately, it is a satisfaction issue. We are not happy in God so we look for satisfaction in stuff.

In his book *The High Price of Materialism*, psychologist Tim Kasser details the years he and his team spent collecting, studying and analyzing data on the intersection of high materialistic values and personal well-being of teens and adults from a wide range of backgrounds. The question they desired to answer was, "What happens psychologically when a person feels that making money and having possessions are relatively high in the pantheon of values?"[11]

The results aren't pretty.

According to Kasser, high materialistic values don't lead to happiness and personal satisfaction. In fact, people who place a high value on wealth and possessions are emptier, more frantic, report deep insecurity and fragile self-worth, have low self-esteem and increased anxiety levels, are at greater risk for depression, experience more frequent somatic irritations, experience lower psychological

---

11. Tim Kasser, *The High Price of Materialism*, 6.

and personal well-being, and have impoverished relationships. They are also less empathic and generous. They are restless, even feeling distress during sleep. Their materialistic values do not cure their insecurity but may work in raising it. Wealth fails to create a meaningful life. In short, "What stands out across the studies is a simple fact: people who strongly value the pursuit of wealth and possessions report lower psychological well-being than those who are less concerned with such aims."[12]

Not the kind of life you want, is it?

Discontentment causes materialism, but materialism causes greater levels of discontentment. A materialistic lifestyle places a burden on the human soul because after you acquire more possessions, you have to work hard to maintain them. You have to constantly fix, insure, manage, renew, upgrade. Extra management costs money and creates an enormous amount of stress and anxiety. Personally, I never worry about my yacht, Lamborghini or mansion, quite simply because I do not own a yacht, Lamborghini or mansion. We see the benefits of material possessions but fail to account for their inevitable burdens.

A need is something that is necessary for survival. God promises to provide for our *needs* but not our *greeds*. Jesus taught his disciples to pray for daily bread, not for daily Parmesan Risotto with Roasted Shrimp. Consumer culture tells us that many of our greeds are needs when they aren't. God is a loving and gracious Father who does spoil us from time to time with desired luxuries, but these are not promised. Often we don't doubt God's provision for our needs, but we question him because he hasn't given us our desires. But God knows best. Trust that God will not only provide, but also that he knows *what* to provide. Trust God's sovereignty, but also trust his wisdom.

Ross Douthat argues that, "The stringency of Christianity's sexual teachings gets most of the press, but the commandment

---

12. Ibid., 5.

against avarice [greed], if taken seriously, can be the faith's most difficult by far."[13]

How can you avoid greed?

Pursuing Contentment with Wealth

Asceticism is the avoidance of pleasure for spiritual reasons. Christians are not ascetics. God created pleasure and as long as you follow his rules, you are free to enjoy. Paul rebukes pleasure-killers in 1 Timothy when he says some "will depart from the faith by devoting themselves to deceitful spirits and teachings of demons" (1 Tim. 4:1). Whoa, teachings of demons. Serious language. Like witchcraft, voodoo, sorcery? No. Apparently they "forbid marriage and require abstinence from foods that God created to be received with thanksgiving" (4:3). They were telling people that they couldn't get married and have sex and enjoy certain foods because doing so was unspiritual. Paul calls this teaching demonic.

Something similar could be said, although in a less severe manner, about those who have a negative view about wealth. We've already seen that the desire and acquisition of wealth creates serious temptations, but here's how you can honor God with the wealth entrusted to you:

> As for the rich in this present age, charge them not to be haughty, nor to set their hopes on the uncertainty of riches, but on God, who richly provides us with everything to enjoy. They are to do good, to be rich in good works, to be generous and ready to share, thus storing up treasure for themselves as a good foundation for the future, so that they may take hold of that which is truly life (1 Tim. 6:17-19).

If you make over $34,000 per year, you're among the richest one percent of the people in the world. Live in the Western part of the world? Then you are likely rich. Here are some applications from Paul's admonitions.

---

13. Ross Douthat, *Bad Religion*, 190.

First, don't be arrogant or "haughty." Wealth and arrogance tend to coexist. But they shouldn't, at least not for Christians. It can be easy to view your money and material possessions and say, "My power and the might of my hand have gotten me this wealth," (Deut. 8:17) when you can't even breathe without God's help, let alone make money. *God* is the one who gives you your talents and spiritual gifts. *God* is the one who gives you your opportunities. *God* is the one who decided that you would live in the twenty-first century and be the benefactor of modern prosperity. Although God's enabling power doesn't undermine personal diligence, everything we own ultimately derives from God.

Second, don't put your hope in wealth. Paul's teaching aligns with the teachings of Jesus who speaks of the "deceitfulness" of riches (Mark 4:19), and the psalmist who warns, "If riches increase, set not your heart on them" (Ps. 62:10). Why? Because they're bad? No. Because they're uncertain. There's no guarantee that you'll get wealth nor keep it if you do. After providing warnings not to put your hope in wealth because it's uncertain, Paul says to put your hope "on God," intentionally contrasting the uncertainty of wealth with the certainty of God.

Giving your money to God's kingdom purposes is a demonstrable sign that you're not putting your hope in wealth. So contribute regularly, cheerfully and sacrificially to the work of God in your midst. Take care of your immediate family, give to your local church and be generous toward Christian organizations and individuals. Cultivating contentment is packed with paradoxes and here is one of them: you grow in contentment not by keeping what you have but by giving it away.

Third, Paul doesn't say that if you're rich you need to give away all your money to charity, but rather says that God "richly provides us with everything to enjoy." John Frame reminds us that "Scripture does not condemn the expenditure of money for relaxation, for entertainment, or even for the consumption of luxuries. But these must be balanced by a concern for others and for one's own future well-being."[14] God is not sadistic and stingy, wanting to only deprive his people. We don't serve a cheap, penny-pinching God who wants us to feel guilty for every second we laugh or have fun. God, instead, commands the enjoyment of wealth because he is a good Father who wants his children to enjoy the pleasures he created and because personal enjoyment of wealth acknowledges that it came from God in the first place. What has God blessed you with—a vacation home, a successful career, an ample supply of money? Enjoy it. Even the ability to enjoy the wealth God entrusts to you is from God, for "Everyone also to whom God has given wealth and possessions and power to enjoy them . . . this is the gift of God" (Eccles. 5:19).

Fourth, bless others with your wealth. You are to "do good," be "rich in good works" and be "generous and ready to share." Part of what it means to enjoy your wealth is to allow others to enjoy it, too. God provides for your benefit, but not for your benefit alone. His generosity toward you should overflow into generosity toward others —specifically, by meeting needs. Through generosity, you store up for yourself imperishable treasures in heaven, something Jesus encourages his disciples to do (Matt. 6:20). When you distribute your resources to advance the work of God, you give away what's not yours to get what you can't lose.[15]

Consider the resources you have and then ask, "How can I use these resources to bless others?" Can you host a small group at your apartment? Can you allow someone in need to live with you? Hospitality is a crucial teaching in the New Testament (1 Pet. 4:9; 1 Tim. 3:2; Titus 1:8), and John even rebukes someone for not wanting to be hospitable (3 John 9-10). Homes were commonly used for ministry in the book of Acts and "no one said that any of the things that belonged to him was his own, but they had everything in common" (Acts 4:32). The early Church generously shared their possessions, making a great impact on those who

---

14. John Frame, *The Doctrine of the Christian Life*, 806.
15. I'm playing off a Jim Elliot quote who says, "He is no fool who gives what he cannot keep to gain that which he cannot lose."

noticed (Acts 2:42-47). A good test to determine how well we understand that our assets are from God is how often we use them to bless others.

A friend of mine is a former pastor in a wealthy church. One question he often received from his church members was, "Should I tithe from my gross income or from my net income?" His response was blunt: "You should seek to be the kind of Christian who doesn't ask those kinds of questions." His point, and the New Testament's point too, I think, is that our giving should not be restricted to a certain percentage for all seasons of life, but should be characterized by generosity.

Adopt a simple lifestyle. We need only the basics for contentment. In his commentary on the Pastoral Epistles, George Knight says, "Whatever exceeds these basics can be gratefully received and enjoyed . . . but should never be conceived as a necessity so that it can destroy true contentment when it is lacking."[16] There's nothing wrong with having or enjoying luxuries, but problems arise when we feel entitled to them or when we think we need more than the necessities for contentment. Adopting a modest lifestyle will better position you to experience contentment.

The Rich King who Became Poor for You

Paul writes to the Corinthians about giving money and mentions the church in Macedonia as an example:

> for in a severe test of affliction, their abundance of joy and their extreme poverty have overflowed in a wealth of generosity on their part. For they gave according to their means, as I can testify, and beyond their means, of their own accord, begging us earnestly for the favor of taking part in the relief of the saints . . ." (2 Cor. 8:2-4).

The Macedonian church didn't let personal suffering stop them from giving money to God's kingdom causes, and they didn't just give 10 percent. They gave beyond their means. Usually ministry leaders

16. George W. Knight III, *The Pastoral Epistles* (Grand Rapids: William B. Eerdmans, 1999), 255.

have to make an emotional appeal for Christians to give, but the Macedonians did not need an appeal because *they* were the ones begging to give, not out of their abundance, but out of their poverty. They are the flagship example of a generous church. When it comes to generosity, it's hard to find a better example to model.

But there is one.

After building his case about the exemplary giving of the Macedonians, Paul writes, "For you know the grace of our Lord Jesus Christ, that though he was rich, yet for your sake he became poor, so that you by his poverty might become rich" (2 Cor. 8:9). Jesus was rich, Paul says. This richness doesn't mean financially, but instead is a reference to his preexistent state in heaven, where Jesus was worshipped by angels and enjoyed perfect fellowship among the members of the Trinity. Authority, respect, honor, glory. Jesus had it all and had it perfectly. But before there was a star or before you were a twinkle in your mother's eyes, the second person of the Trinity, Jesus Christ, agreed to leave his majestic state in heaven to become poor for your sake. Poor, similar to rich, doesn't refer to Jesus' financial or economic status during his earthly life, but rather to his incarnation. Paul is talking about Jesus leaving heaven to take on human flesh—the one who "emptied himself, by taking the form of a servant," and even "humbled himself by becoming obedient to the point of death, even death on a cross" (Phil. 2:7-8). Now, the work of Christ makes you rich. Not financially, of course. Paul is keeping in step with the metaphor: the Corinthians' richness—and consequently everyone in Christ—means all the blessings enjoyed as being part of the people of God.

Although the Macedonian church serves as a helpful example, the ultimate example of generous giving flows from Jesus Christ.

Do you struggle with generosity? Do you find hospitality difficult? Are you discontent with the amount of wealth you own? Remember Jesus Christ (2 Tim. 2:8). Meditate on his sacrifice for you. Consider his incarnation, his perfect life, death and resurrection. Ask him through prayer to change you and help you to grow in generosity. Let your generosity flow not from compulsion or a desire to be needed, but as a response to what Christ has done for you.

Chapter 5
Pain and Suffering

"If I should suffer need, and go unclothed, and be in poverty, make my heart prize thy love, know it, be constrained by it, though I be denied all blessings."
— Puritan prayer

"For all whom the Lord has adopted and received among the number of his children must prepare themselves for a tough, difficult life, full of toils and countless troubles." — John Calvin

He described himself as shy, timid, and awkward. But his stride and speech in public was characterized with remarkable confidence. His personality was dominant, his thinking razor sharp, and his impact on Protestant Christians undeniable, even by his critics. He was a brilliant communicator of God's Word, a prolific preacher and writer. His famous book on the Christian faith is still being widely read hundreds of years after his death. If you read his words (and not someone else's words about his words) and study his life (and not someone else's thoughts about his life), you'll gain a deeper appreciation for John Calvin—a man mightily used by God, but who suffered deeply.[1]

Calvin lived and worked with a "brilliant mind in a failing body."[2] He experienced unusual writing success but also a tremendous amount of tragedy, persecution, conflict, criticism and betrayal. He was constantly in transit, running in danger for his life, seeking to escape political and religious turmoil. Mobs would sometimes show up at his house, firing their guns, and threatening to throw him in the river. Completely zealous for the Lord, he often stayed up until

---

1. Bruce Gordon, *Calvin* (New Haven: Yale University Press, 2011).
2. Ibid, 144.

midnight in pursuit of the knowledge of God. Today he is the subject of both unhealthy praise and ignorant criticism.

Calvin was no stranger to suffering. He ate and slept little. He had multiple childhood weaknesses that he did not overcome in adulthood. His eyes were destroyed through reading by candlelight. At a young age, he found himself operating under a monastic regime which produced incredible self-discipline, but also tendencies to overwork—unhealthy habits that led to his death. Calvin suffered with chronic asthma, migraines, pleurisy, insomnia, kidney stones, hemorrhoids, gallstones, bleeding from the stomach, severe arthritis and frequent influenza accompanied by raging fevers. He had to be carried to and from his pulpit for his last sermon. He lived with a fractured body. He was acquainted with pain.

Calvin married a woman named Idelette de Burr who was converted through his preaching. They experienced the pain of miscarriage and babies dying in infancy, and were unable to have any children. Idelette died young, less than nine years after marriage. Calvin never remarried. His enemies said God cursed him by denying him children. They also said his wife died of boredom and, after his death, his critics named their dogs after him.

Calvin's response to suffering is exemplary. How did he endure amidst his pain? Through an unshakeable confidence in the sovereignty and goodness of God. On his deathbed, his friend Theodore Beza heard him say, "Thou, O Lord, bruisest me; but it is enough for me that it is thy hand."[3]

Calvin was aware of his intellectual genius, but also recognized that God did not design him to have full understanding of all the reasons behind his suffering. For Calvin, it was enough for him to know his trials were under the hand of God.

Contentment and Suffering

For most people, the natural reaction to suffering is resentment, not contentment. Unlike secular methods, in the Christian faith, we

---

3. Quoted in Michael Horton, *Calvin on the Christian Life: Glorifying and Enjoying God Forever* (Wheaton: Crossway, 2014), 262.

have a God who provides supernatural strength during seasons of suffering. The Scriptural passage that deals most with contentment in suffering is in 2 Corinthians. It's one of Paul's most personal letters. 2 Corinthians is about the relationship between suffering and the power of God in Paul's ministry. Paul responds to his opponents who criticized him and questioned his apostleship because Paul suffered so much. Can he really be an Apostle of God if he's constantly suffering? But suffering and Christian faithfulness are not incompatible. It's through weakness and suffering—not strength and success—that Christ's power shines most brightly.

Paul writes about a man who went to heaven and is prohibited to speak about his heavenly experience (2 Cor. 12:2). The person Paul speaks about is himself. But since this heavenly trip could produce pride in Paul, God gives Paul a thorn in his flesh. This is where we learn about contentment in suffering:

> So to keep me from becoming conceited because of the surpassing greatness of the revelations, a thorn was given me in the flesh, a messenger of Satan to harass me, to keep me from becoming conceited. Three times I pleaded with the Lord about this, that it should leave me. But he said to me, "My grace is sufficient for you, for my power is made perfect in weakness." Therefore I will boast all the more gladly of my weaknesses, so that the power of Christ may rest upon me. For the sake of Christ, then, I am content with weaknesses, insults, hardships, persecutions, and calamities. For when I am weak, then I am strong (2 Cor. 12:7-10).

Purposeful Thorns

Paul says, "a thorn was given me in the flesh." Thorn here means something pointed, like a stake. It's something that causes serious frustration. A thorn is not something that annoys you, like a slow metabolism. Instead, a thorn is something in your life that you can't control which causes you ongoing pain that you would remove if you had the power to do so. Sometimes we don't understand what God is doing with our pain. Sometimes we overread what God might be doing with our pain. And still other times, we have some measure of understanding about what God may be doing with our pain. Paul had clarity about why God sent a thorn into his flesh: humility. To emphasize the thorn's specific purpose in his life, Paul twice uses the expression: "to keep me from becoming conceited." The thorn was God's means to prevent Paul from pride.

Pride is a serious sin. It's what got Satan kicked out of heaven. It's what keeps people from God. And it's a character deficiency that can lead to self-destruction. Since God loves his children and doesn't want them to self-destruct, and since the sin of pride so easily creeps into the human heart, God sees fit on his timing and in his way to occasionally humble us through God-approved thorns.

Paul was not beyond the need of learning contentment (Phil. 4:10-13), and he was not beyond the need of learning humility. God disciplines everyone he loves. He sends each one of his children to the desert from time to time to wean us of self-reliance, increase our hope in heaven, and prevent or remove pride from our hearts.

To ask why God allows suffering is a fair question. But what if we twisted the wording? What if we asked, "What would happen if God *didn't* allow suffering?" The results wouldn't be as good as you might think. If God didn't send an occasional thorn, you would be less inclined to practice dependence. You may stop going to church. You wouldn't read your Bible and pray as much. You'd likely lack empathy, become prideful and spiritually lethargic, and fall into idolatry. "Prone to wander, Lord, I feel it, Prone to leave the God I love," goes the famous hymn. Thorns are preventive. They keep you from wandering from God.

Unbelievers view suffering as an unwanted disruption, but believers look past the inconvenience of pain and experience a deeper sense of God's presence. Those who respond well to suffering become more resilient, grow in godliness, and set good examples. On the other side, those who haven't suffered or who don't respond well to suffering usually become shallow or bitter. Pain and suffering awaken us from our comfortable Christian lives and force us to seek God for strength and endurance. I wish there was a different way, but as long as we live in this fallen world, it's through purposeful thorns that God keeps you dependent on him.

God's Fatherly Hand Behind Your Suffering

The question about suffering is often posed like this: Why does God *allow* suffering? That's fine if you prefer "allow." I understand its use. But for me, "allow" in relation to God's involvement in my suffering doesn't quite capture God's power and goodness and wisdom behind my trials. It makes God seem remotely involved in my pain, passively allowing this or that to affect my life. For me, words like "send" and "give" better help me to see God's hand in my pain. Paul says "a thorn was given me in the flesh." *Given.* Of course, God is not the author of evil, and pain is the result of our sinful flesh, the enemy and this world. But let's not act like God is removed from a single ounce of our suffering, as if he didn't see it coming. We inadequately capture God's heart when we believe he is remote in our pain. Similar to a good earthly father who disciplines his children, God sends pain for your good to help you experience that "all things, in fact, come to us not by chance but from his fatherly hand."[4]

Paul doesn't say what the thorn is. Consider the wisdom of God in inspiring Paul to write "thorn" rather than Paul's specific pain. Why? As others have said, it enables you to relate to Paul. Since Paul writes "thorn" without specific identification, it makes all Christians everywhere who have a proverbial thorn in their flesh empathize with Paul. The ambiguity leads to connection with Paul's suffering.

The thorn comes from God, but Satan is involved: "a messenger of Satan to harass me." The primary cause is God; the secondary cause is Satan. Often, God works through others. Satan cannot move an inch to the left or right without God's permission. When Satan wounds, he is not hindering God's plan; he's furthering God's plan. The thorn served to prevent Paul from conceit, though this is not what Satan wanted![5]

---

4.   Heidelberg Catechism, Q 27
5.   *New Bible Commentary*, 1204.

Think about Job. The Scriptures teach that Job was a blameless and upright man, extremely godly, and highly prosperous: "And the Lord said to Satan, 'Have you considered my servant Job, that there is none like him on the earth, a blameless and upright man, who fears God and turns away from evil?'" (Job 1:8). The narrative continues: "And the Lord said to Satan, 'Behold, all that he has is in your hand. Only against him do not stretch out your hand'" (Job 1:12).

You probably know the story. Job experiences a succession of tragedies. We don't know all the reasons behind God's plan for Job. But we do know Job's personal testimony has encouraged billions of Christians over the centuries. Such is the wisdom and power of God that he can bring about good from painful tragedies.

Do you have a thorn in your flesh? Take heart. It's not accidental. God has a specific purpose for it, although you may not know what it is. God sees the end from the beginning, but we only see past and present. You won't always know the purpose behind your thorns, but you know it's not because God doesn't love you.[6] God will never leave or abandon you, and he sees every tear and hears every cry. "God wants your trust more than your understanding," said New Testament scholar D.A. Carson, as I listened to him speak in person about suffering. That line has stayed with me through the years. I've used it in sermons and it's provided an "aha" moment for others. We want relief, but God wants trust. I'll repeat Calvin's words: "Thou, O Lord, bruisest me; but it is enough for me that it is thy hand."

The Grace of Lament

Paul writes: "Three times I pleaded with the Lord about this, that it should leave me" (2 Cor. 12:8). Paul strongly pleads with the Lord not once, not twice, but three times: "Lord, please remove this thorn. Lord, please remove this thorn. Lord, please remove this thorn." Paul desperately wanted healing. But God denied his request.

---

6. Tim Keller, *The Reason for God: Belief in An Age of Skepticism* (New York: Penguin Books, 2009), 31.

You might feel discouraged after praying for the removal of your thorn to no avail. You may even wonder if God is listening to you. Charles Spurgeon, a well-known Baptist preacher from the 1800s, once cried out to God in his pain in a desperate prayer:

> I have found it a blessing, in my own experience, to plead with God that I am his child. Some months ago, when I was suffering with an extreme pain, so bad that I could not bear it without crying out, I asked everyone to go out from my room, and leave me alone. Then I had nothing I could say to God but this:
>
> 'You are my Father, and I am your child; and you, as a Father, are gentle and full of mercy. I could not bear my child to suffer as you make me suffer; and if I saw him tormented as I am now, I would do what I could to help him and put my arms under him to sustain him. Will you hide your face from me, my Father? Will you still lay on me your heavy hand, and not give to me your smile? . . . If he be a Father, let him show himself to be a Father.'
>
> This is what I prayed; and when those who cared for me came back I had courage to tell them that I shall never have such agony again from this moment, for God has heard my prayer. I bless God that relief came, and the most terrible pain never returned. Faith mastered it by laying hold upon God in His own revealed character—the character in which, in our darkest hour, we are best able to appreciate him.[7]

Spurgeon got relief. Let this encourage you to pray fervently in your pain. But not everyone gets relief from their pain in this life. Paul pleaded three times, not four. That means Paul ceased praying for healing. Sometimes we wonder if or how to pray when our specific prayer requests are denied. Should I keep praying for relief or pray differently? I don't always know the answer. There aren't easy solutions to complex problems. But we do know we have the Psalms as a guide. When we don't know how to pray, we practice the grace of lament.

In his book *Dark Clouds, Deep Mercy: Discovering the Grace of Lament*, Mark Vroegop defines a lament as: "A loud cry, a howl, or a passionate expression of grief." Lament is "A prayer in pain that

---

7. Charles Spurgeon's sermon, "Heaven's Nurse Children" No. 1021.

leads to trust." It involves two questions: (1) Where are you, God? (2) If you love me, why is this happening?[8]

There are 150 Psalms in the Bible and around a third of them are laments. They often follow this fourfold pattern: (1) Turn to God in prayer; (2) Voice your concerns to God in specific and blunt language; (3) Present your request; (4) Trust God with the results.[9]

Lament is not the time to be polished or professional. It's not the time to "get it right." When lamenting, we put away all polish, eloquence and showiness. Just start with what's on your heart (even if it's messy) and go from there. When lamenting, we follow in the footsteps of Jesus: "In the days of his flesh, Jesus offered up prayers and supplications, with loud cries and tears, to him who was able to save him from death, and he was heard because of his reverence" (Heb. 5:7). As a result of Christ's example, we draw near to the throne of grace and receive supernatural help (Heb. 4:16).

The Blessing of Weakness

A "weakness is a state of inadequacy, or insufficiency, in relation to some standard or ideal to which we desire to conform."[10] It's a personal limitation to complete a human task. A weakness can be physical, mental, intellectual, emotional, or spiritual. And, of course, nobody desires weakness. We desire strength. We want to be known as put-together people. Strength is a sign of status, like wealth and attractiveness. And strength is obviously good. God told Joshua multiple times to be strong (Josh. 1:9), and Paul told his readers to "be strong in the Lord" (Eph. 6:10). But God's views of strength and weakness and the culture's are incongruent.

Culturally speaking, you should avoid your weaknesses. Discover your strengths and leverage those to get ahead in life. We have been culturally trained to believe the good life is one of ease and comfort. And acknowledging your weaknesses is antithetical to the good life.

---

8.   Mark Vroegop, *Dark Clouds, Deep Mercy: Discovering the Grace of Lament* (Wheaton: Crossway, 2019), 28.

9.   Ibid, 29.

10.   J.I. Packer, *Weakness is the Way: Life with Christ Our Strength* (Wheaton: Crossway, 2018), 49.

I recount the two years working in a supplement retail store where I sold thousands of people supplements so they would no longer look or feel weak. Once I served a customer who had an unusually strong external appearance, and he openly shared his desire for a muscular exterior was rooted in his childhood memories where he felt weak. When I was in undergraduate school, I remember being trained to say "I'm a perfectionist" if ever asked in a job interview about my weaknesses; that way I could mix a strength with a weakness. But Christians need not hide from their weaknesses.

Earlier in the book of 2 Corinthians, Paul acknowledges a criticism from his opponents who called him "weak": "For they say, 'His letters are weighty and strong, but his bodily presence is weak, and his speech of no account'" (2 Cor. 10:10). This is a hurtful criticism. But Paul doesn't get defensive. He doesn't need human affirmation. In fact, Paul admits to his critics that they're right. Paul *is* weak. But his weaknesses are an asset, not a liability because it's in weakness where Christ manifests his power. Instead of hiding from his weaknesses, Paul says, "Therefore I will boast all the more gladly of my weaknesses, so that the power of Christ may rest upon me" (2 Cor. 12:9). Most Christians try to hide from their weaknesses, but Paul boasts in his.

The strengths that you have are given by God, but so are your weaknesses. We don't think about this enough. Your weaknesses are not an accident, but gifts from God as a means for deeper fellowship with him. When feeling weak, our temptation is to hide, lie (or mix a truth with a lie, which is more powerful), resign to passivity, run from God, or overcompensate by speaking too much about our strengths. How many times have we arrived at church seeming put together but really we were living in sin? Or how many times have we told a "small" lie when asked about a personal insecurity? But we've got it all wrong. Instead of running from our weaknesses, we should acknowledge them. Doing so is a countercultural expression of dependence. It creates self-awareness and cultivates humility. It's also liberating. We'll never be okay with admitting our weaknesses as long as we crave the approval of others. We are saved by grace, not by our strengths.

In weakness, we experience the power of God in a way that we don't with our strengths. God's power doesn't shine in human strength because it's unclear whether the shining is from your strength or God's. But when death strikes, or when you're sick and tired, or when you have chronic pain, or when you're about to embark on a task that seems too difficult—these are the moments when Christ's power is manifested. Relying on God in your weakness is the way to experience the power of Christ. Weakness is a prerequisite for power. The greater the weakness or the difficulty, the more clearly God's power is displayed.

Power in Weakness

Paul is unhealed, but not unheard. God denies Paul's thorn removal request, but gives him something better—his grace. "But he said to me, 'My grace is sufficient for you, for my power is made perfect in weakness'" (2 Cor. 12:9). God's grace toward his people is a demonstration of his benevolent character. It's where God shows you favor and loving-kindness as the recipient of his care. We sometimes experience pain and toss up a quick prayer for healing, and then get mad at God for not quickly healing us. We're impatient. We'd rather quickly get healed instead of wrestle with God and grow in character. Although desiring healing is normal, being quickly healed from every pain and being quickly removed from every trial removes the opportunity for you to experience the precious presence and power of God in your pain.

But here's where the idea of contentment in suffering is powerfully revealed in this passage. The Lord says to Paul, "My grace is sufficient for you" (2 Cor. 12:9). In the New Testament orginal langauge, what does "sufficient" here mean? You might be able to guess it at this point: it means "be content." This is the key: *The path to contentment in suffering is through God's empowering grace.* God's empowering grace is an active, ongoing and presently available reality. It's a constant and never-ending supply of supernatural strength.

Paul doesn't run from his weaknesses. He boasts in them, and even says he's content with "weaknesses, insults, hardships, persecutions, and calamities" (2 Cor. 12:10). When Paul says, "the power of Christ may rest upon me" (2 Cor. 12:9), it reminds us of God's presence in the Old Testament tabernacle or God pitching his tent with the Israelites (Exod. 40:34). Tabernacle (or "tent of meeting") means "dwelling place." It's where God dwelt with his people for a time. Just like in the Old Testament when God makes his presence especially felt in the tabernacle, or today when we gather for corporate worship and especially feel God's presence with our church family, Jesus "tabernacles," so to speak, with his people in their pain, and makes his presence especially felt.

Paul's contentment in weakness is not because he enjoys suffering, but because it's God's power in Paul's weaknesses, not Paul's experience in heaven that will be the platform God uses to showcase his glory. This is the main point of 2 Corinthians 12:1-12 and Paul's self-defense throughout 2 Corinthians. Instead of self-authenticating his ministry through success, Paul validates his ministry through God's power in his weakness.

When Jesus' Prayer Request Was Denied

Paul is not the only one who prayed for relief three times. Jesus also did in the Garden of Gethsemane when he prayed for the cup of God's wrath to be removed. But God the Father denied his request. And Paul was not the only one who experienced weakness. Later in 2 Corinthians, Paul says Jesus was "crucified in weakness" (2 Cor. 13:4). Although Paul's thorn is a powerful example of God's power shining brightly in weakness, the cross of Christ is the ultimate example of God's power shining brightly in weakness. The Son of God was on a blood-stained tree, beaten and battered beyond recognition in public humiliation. God lost, it seemed. It was over. Until it wasn't. Three days later, Jesus victoriously defeated the grave. What appeared as weakness secured the salvation of God's people.

Coming Down: The Glorious Restoration

I felt profoundly homesick during my first semester of college. I assumed the homesickness would eventually leave, and it did. But at the start of every semester, for four and a half years, the homesickness returned. I just couldn't wait to get home during scheduled school breaks. Once during spring break, I was driving so fast to get home and blaring the music as loud as I could that I got a speeding ticket. Although the homesickness was painful, knowing an opportunity to go back home was just months away provided the strength I needed to endure the distance from home.

Most Christians rightly view heaven as a perfect paradise with no more suffering or sin. But heaven is not just consolation but restoration.[11] What do I mean? When we think about the new heaven and new earth, we often think about "going up." But the first two verses in Revelation 21 teaches the New Creation is coming down: "Then I saw a new heaven and a new earth, for the first heaven and the first earth had passed away, and the sea was no more. And I saw the holy city, new Jerusalem, *coming down* out of heaven from God, prepared as a bride adorned for her husband" (Rev. 21:1-2). Contrary to popular Christian belief, when Jesus comes back, he's not going to burn up everything on Earth, as if everything we do and create now is useless. When Jesus ushers in the New Creation, everything will not be burned, but restored.

This restoration includes your life. It includes your unanswered questions. And it includes your sorrow and suffering. You will not only experience the perfect paradise once you enter into the new heavens, but you will also be restored with everything lost or broken. You will finally learn the "why" behind your trials, and the restorative nature of heaven works in such a way that you will experience greater joy in heaven as a result of your pain on earth. "This means that every horrible thing that ever happened will not only be undone and repaired but will in some way make the eventual

---

11.   Tim Keller, *The Reason for God*, 32.

90

glory and joy even greater."[12] Somehow, in a way that our finite minds cannot now fully understand, the new heavens and new earth will never cease to be an endless and ever-increasing paradise of joy where everything will make sense, and "everything sad is going to come untrue and it will somehow be *greater* for having once been broken and lost."[13]

---

12. Ibid, 32.
13. Ibid, 33.

Chapter 6
Success and Work

"And do you seek great things for yourself? Seek them not . . ."
— Jeremiah 45:5

"Our aspirations entitle us to nothing." — Dan Doriani

Billy Graham was one of the most famous public figures ever. He preached the gospel of Jesus Christ to over 200 million people in more than 180 countries and reached millions more through books, radio broadcasts and other forms of media. Graham was friends with a large number of high-profile international leaders, often spending time with American presidents and other widely recognized celebrities. He's been labeled as "America's Pastor" and is undeniably one of the most prominent evangelists in the history of Christianity.

He also got famous by accident.

The year was 1949. Graham was in his early thirties. At a rough spiritual patch in his life, Graham spent weeks in a crisis of faith doubting the reliability of the Scriptures, but God delivered Graham from his spiritual turmoil with vigor to evangelize. This led Graham to Los Angeles, California to preach at crusades. At this point in the evangelist's life, he mustered a small to medium-sized platform, even serving as a college president by the time he turned thirty. He enjoyed *some* success. He didn't spring from nowhere. But Graham wasn't a household name yet. That changed, however, during the middle of this preaching trip. There was initially modest attendance during the crusades, but suddenly the crusades were overflowing with people and reporters and Graham became a celebrity overnight.

What happened?

Two notable journalists, William Randolph Hearst and Henry Luce, leveraged their influence to propel Graham into the spotlight. Luce used his power to put Graham on the cover of *Time Magazine.* Hearst sent a telegram to his newspaper editors with two words, the now famous instructions, "Puff Graham." Essentially, Hearst declared, "Make Billy Graham famous." The exposure was massive, causing the crusades to extend for an additional four weeks, with Graham's popularity rapidly rising. Sending a message by telegram and placing someone on a magazine cover seems archaic, even abstract, since we're well into the twenty-first century, but this was at a time when newspapers and magazines were a popular form of media.

These two events propelled Graham to fame. The Billy Graham Association was founded the following year, when Graham began his major crusades all over the world. The rest, as they say, is history.

The crazy thing? Graham never met Hearst, never had a conversation with him, didn't ask him to do this favor, and never had an opportunity to thank him. The reporters weren't drawn to Graham for religious reasons. No, they puffed Graham because they thought Graham could help *them* with their anticommunist views. But God had other plans in mind when he used the motives and actions of two reporters to give Graham a platform. No wonder Proverbs says that "The king's heart is a stream of water in the hand of the Lord; he turns it wherever he will" (Prov. 21:1). One way that God gives you favor in this life is by giving you favor with influential people. And often, God gives the greatest success to those who don't seek it.

Billy Graham didn't seek the spotlight; the spotlight sought him. He just so happened to be in Los Angeles and two journalists who just so happened to dislike communism just so happened to be drawn to him and they just so happened to use their influence to make Graham famous. This "just so happened" language is used by the author of Ruth who writes that Ruth "just so happened" to glean in one of the fields belonging to Boaz (Ruth 2:3). This one seemingly accidental event led to a beautiful love story. But there are no accidents. There's no such thing as luck, coincidence or chance. Every step you take is planned by God. Even the most seemingly minuscule events are governed by him. Just because something seems small and incidental to you doesn't mean that God isn't working behind the scenes. This is the echo of providence—God's mysterious hand working through everything.

Graham's outlier success is not something you can manufacture no matter how hard you try, how many people you meet, how many books you read, how many degrees you obtain, or how gifted you are. Don't minimize your effort when seeking success. But a Christian perspective on success recognizes that ultimately all success comes from God.

The man who doubted the Bible for a season started saying, "The Bible says . . ." to reach millions for Christ.[1]

Defining Success Without Being Hyper-Spiritual[2]

We tend to define success in one of two ways. The first is to define success as faithfulness. "As long as you're faithful, you're successful," people say. I respect the view that believes success is faithfulness to God. To define success as faithfulness, however, may be an oversimplification because it conveniently removes you from being personally held accountable for *some* measure of results. What you think "faithful" means and what I think it means may be totally different. If a person faithfully posts edifying Christian material on social media daily, but nobody likes, shares, comments, or follows them, are they successful at social media?

The first definition is better than the second one, which views success the way the world does, through money, numbers, status, influence, etc. This definition is problematic for obvious reasons.

---

1. John D. Woodbridge, Frank A. James III, *Church History, Volume Two: From Pre-Reformation to the Present Day: The Rise and Growth of the Church in its Cultural, Intellectual, and Political Context* (Grand Rapids: Zondervan, 2013), 810-12.

2. Tim Keller, *Center Church: Doing Balanced, Gospel-Centered Ministry in Your City* (Grand Rapids: Zondervan, 2012), 13-14.

"As I read," Tim Keller says, "reflected, and taught, I came to the conclusion that a more biblical theme for ministerial evaluation than either success or faithfulness is *fruitfulness*."[3] The context is Christian ministry, but the broader principle applies to success as a general term for Christians: fruitfulness is success. Fruitfulness is work that creates value for others by demonstrably leading to increased well-being of the recipient. It happens when people are blessed by your efforts, like when someone grows in Christ under your ministry, or when someone tells you your writing has inspired them to deeper service. Defining success as fruitfulness is a preferable middle ground because it keeps an appropriate amount of accountability on you to work hard, but it liberates you from having worldly standards of measurement for your work.

Success is Out of Your Hands (Sort of)

God has already planned out each one of your days (Ps. 139:16). This includes the amount of vocational success you'll experience. What a tremendous source of comfort for the ambitious believer. This belief creates contentment as you experience the highs and lows of your vocational endeavors since even rewards and setbacks are planned by an infinitely wise God. And yet, God's plan for your life doesn't minimize your responsibility. God is 100 percent sovereign, but you are 100 percent responsible to work hard. To pit the two against each other is to do something Scripture never does. If our understanding of God's sovereignty leads to passivity, then we've misapplied God's sovereignty.[4] How these work together is a mystery that leads to worship and personal diligence, but never to excuses or complaining. So while major success is somewhat out of your control, ambition is still a prerequisite for success.

---

3. Tim Keller, *Center Church*, 13.
4. Dave Harvey, *Rescuing Ambition*, 85.

Redeeming Ambition (But Not the Demonic Kind)[5]

Ambition is ". . . the instinctual motivation to aspire to things, to make something happen, to have an impact, to count for something in life."[6] While many Christians speak negatively about ambition, the Bible speaks positively about it on a few occasions (e.g., Rom. 15:20-21, 2 Cor. 5:9-11). So ambition is not all bad. Ambition and contentment can coexist.

James K.A. Smith puts it this way:

> . . . the opposite of ambition is not humility; it is sloth, passivity, timidity, and complacency. We sometimes like to comfort ourselves by imagining that the ambitious are prideful and arrogant so that those of us who never risk, never aspire, never launch out into the deep get to wear the moralizing mantle of humility. But this imagining is often just thin cover for a lack of courage, even laziness. Playing it safe isn't humble.[7]

Failing to use your talents for maximum impact is disobedience, not humility (Matt. 25:14-30). Obedience to some of Jesus' commands requires godly ambition. Jesus says, for example: "From everyone who has been given much, much will be demanded" (Luke 12:48 NIV). How can you obey this command if you don't have some kind of inward drive? God expects you to make the most of all he has entrusted to you. Think of the Apostle Paul, who made it his ". . . *ambition* to preach the gospel, not where Christ has already been named" (Rom. 15:20). Ambition is translated as "aim" in 2 Corinthians 5:9 where Paul says: ". . . we make it our *aim* to please him" (2 Cor. 5:9). Sin and ambition are not synonyms and you shouldn't allow passive Christians to guilt trip you for your zeal. I'd rather work with a slightly overly ambitious Christian than a

---

5. I was well served by James K.A Smith's chapter on ambition in *On the Road with St. Augustine.*

6. Dave Harvey, *Rescuing Ambition,* 12

7. James K.A. Smith, *On the Road with Saint Augustine: A Real-World Spirituality for Restless Hearts* (Ada: Brazos Press, 2019), 78.

sluggard. It was William Carey who said: "Expect great things from God. Attempt great things for God."

In our present cultural moment, there is much discussion about an influencer's platform. It's something you stand on to help your message reach more people. It consists of your "visibility, credibility, and community."[8] Ezra, a well-known Old Testament teacher of the Law (credibility) stood on a high wooden platform (visibility) that was built by others (community) (Neh. 8:4-5).[9] Yes, it's ethically permissible for you to build a platform if you have the right goal (God's glory), do it according to God's standard (Bible), and are governed by the right motive (love for God and neighbor).[10] This is a stewardship issue. If God has blessed you with the ability to write and speak and lead and influence people in such a way that glorifies him and helps others, why not try to reach as many people as you can?

You should, however, first prioritize local church influence over online influence. At the very least, unless hindered, you should be in good standing as a member of a local church with a track record of giving and serving. It's wrong to seek faithfulness online but neglect faithfulness in your local church.

Godly ambition is achievable, but ambitious pursuits can go awry quickly. Tasting success can fuel an unhealthy desire for more of it—even if you have to sin to get it. Enter selfish ambition. Shockingly, James calls selfish ambition demonic.

The Half-Brother of Jesus Weighs In

How can you tell if you have selfish ambition? It's usually revealed through *motives, disappointment* and *result of actions:* Why (motives) do I want a platform? How (disappointment) do I respond to vocational failure? What (result of actions) did my actions lead

---

8. Andrew T. Le Peau, *Write Better: A Lifelong Editor on Craft, Art, and Spirituality* (Westmont: IVP, 2019), 229.

9. I'm indebted to Al Hsu for this analogy. Quoted in Andrew T. Le Peau, *Write Better*, 228.

10. Dan Doriani, *Work*, 43.

to? When your dreams are denied or delayed, your true motives spring to the surface.

The blunt half-brother of Jesus said:

> But if you have bitter jealousy and selfish ambition in your hearts, do not boast and be false to the truth. This is not the wisdom that comes down from above, but is earthly, unspiritual, demonic. For where jealousy and selfish ambition exist, there will be disorder and every vile practice (James 3:14-17).

Selfish ambition is "self-seeking pursuits through unfair means."[11] Selfish ambition is a willingness to hurt others for personal gain. None of our actions should originate from selfish ambition, Paul says (Phil. 2:3). It was Satan's selfish ambition that forced him out of heaven (Isa. 14:12-14; Ezek. 28:12-18). A fruit of selfish ambition is an inordinate desire to be noticed. During one period of Augustine's life, he confessed, "I wanted to distinguish myself as an orator for a damnable and conceited purpose, namely delight in human vanity."[12] James doesn't sugarcoat the perilous influence of selfish ambition in a group setting. He doesn't say, "Selfish ambition is a small sin that may cause trouble." He says selfish ambition is demonic and will cause serious division.

Ask yourself: Do I alienate people? Do my actions lead to disunity and division? Do I take advantage of people? Do I only network to take rather than serve?

Jesus overturned the tables in the temple (John 2:13-17), and Phineas executed a couple having sex near the tent of meeting (Num. 25:1-18), but both are commended because they were motivated by God's glory. By contrast, selfish ambition is indicative of misguided zeal. It comes from our sinful nature. But it's also developed by experience. For example, overbearing parents can create perfectionistic tendencies and selfish ambition in adult years.

---

11. BDAG.
12. Quoted in James K.A. Smith, *On the Road with St. Augustine*, 80-81.

We will crave attention if we felt overlooked as a child. Culture, too, tells us all kinds of lies and places a premium on status and achievement. Childhood wounds may compel you to succeed to justify your existence. Being self-motivated is a good thing, but our zeal should be redirected from self and toward Christ.

Why do you long for success? Why do you desire to be seen? One writer proposes the reason is *domination* and *attention*, the desire "to win the crown and be seen doing it."[13] To use spiritual language, our hearts may even yearn for praise, worship and glory. But we were created to worship not to be worshipped. All the success in the world cannot satisfy the deepest longings of your heart. At some point, if we're successful, we stop caring about our craft and only care about producing bigger numbers than the next guy. What starts as a genuine desire to help turns into an unquenchable sinful thirst.

Madonna admits:

> I have an iron will, and all of my will has always been to conquer some horrible feeling of inadequacy... I push past one spell of it and discover myself as a special human being and then I get to another stage and think I'm mediocre and uninteresting... Again and again, my drive in life is from this horrible fear of being mediocre. And that's always pushing me, pushing me. Because even though I've become Somebody, I still have to prove that I'm Somebody. My struggle has never ended and it probably never will.[14]

Fans are fickle. Attention doesn't last. Money comes and goes. The euphoria from accomplishments declines quickly. Eventually, you'll leave all of your work in the hands of another. And most of us will not be remembered 100 years from now. Seeking to find worth from accomplishments is a recipe for spiritual bankruptcy. Only when communion with God becomes our highest pursuit will those gnawing feelings of emptiness fade, and only then will we be able to enjoy success without desperately feeling like we need it. The

---

13.   James K.A. Smith, *On the Road with St. Augustine*, 81.
14.   Quoted in Tim Keller, *Counterfeit Gods*, 72.

attention you desire you already have in Christ. His eyes are never *not* on you (Ps. 139:1-6). When God's love for you in Christ reaches the deep parts of your soul, your inordinate desire to be seen will disappear.

Don't self-isolate to the woods to fight against selfish ambition. Once you get there you'll discover some other sin to tackle. The remedy for selfish ambition, instead, as James says, is to seek wisdom from the God who gives to those who ask in faith (James 1:5-6; 3:17). God's wisdom will make you peaceable, and peace is the remedy for selfish ambition (James 3:18).

Sometimes our motives indicate we should not pursue a particular vocational option. But the sad truth is that life in a fallen world means our motives are often mixed. Wise counsel helps, but despite varied motives, it's still okay to write, speak, post and climb the corporate ladder, knowing that God can use you despite imperfect motives.[15] Only in Christianity do we have a God who is so big, so powerful, that he can use our imperfect motives and pathetic effort for his glory.

Corinthians and Christian Celebrities

The church at Corinth might be the most infamous church of all time: litigation was filed (1 Cor. 6:1-11), a guy had sex with his stepmom (1 Cor. 5:1), and someone got drunk at the communion table (1 Cor. 11:21). Add to this dysfunction the factionalism that sprang out of unhealthy attachment to Christian leaders. Amazingly, despite knowledge of these bizarre issues, Paul addresses the church as saints (1 Cor. 1:2) and thanks God for them (1 Cor. 1:4).

Nonetheless, Paul sharply rebukes the church for these issues, including favoring Christian leaders. The context is found in chapter three. Some in the church favored Paul over Apollos and vice versa (1 Cor. 3:4). Then Paul says in verses five to nine:

---

15. James K.A. Smith, *On the Road with Saint Augustine*, 91.

What then is Apollos? What is Paul? Servants through whom you believed, as the Lord assigned to each. I planted, Apollos watered, but God gave the growth.[7] So neither he who plants nor he who waters is anything, but only God who gives the growth. He who plants and he who waters are one, and each will receive his wages according to his labor. For we are God's fellow workers. You are God's field, God's building.

Servants, Not Celebrities

Paul planted the Church. Apollos took it over and pastored it. They were teammates, not opponents; servants, not celebrities. The Corinthians should also see themselves this way and work together to build the Church.

Paul follows the example of the Lord Jesus who did not come to be served but to serve (Mark 10:45). Paul is not displaying fake humility by diminishing the hard work of Apollos and himself. Planting and watering are prerequisites for growth. God doesn't work through inactivity. He works through people, and some deserve to be appropriately recognized. Paul, instead, diverts attention away from man and puts it on God. Planting and watering are done in vain without growth and God is the one who provides the growth. God may use you to bear spiritual fruit, but you still remain utterly dependent on God. In the Church, a person might have more power and gifting, but church members should work with one another, not against one another (1 Cor. 12:12-26).

What does it look like to be a servant?

Let me share this story, from Doug Nichols[16]:

> In 1966 I joined Operation Mobilization for a year of ministry in France, but spent two years in India instead. While in London that summer, at the one-month OM orientation, I volunteered to work on a clean-up crew late one night. Around 12:30am I was sweeping the front steps of the Conference Centre when an older gentleman approached and asked if this was the OM conference.
>
> I told him it was, but most everyone was in bed. He had a small bag with him and was dressed very simply. He said he was

---

16. https://www.epm.org/blog/2009/May/26/a-life-of-humility

attending the conference, so I said, "Let me see if I can find you a place to sleep." Since there were many different age groups at OM, I thought he was an older OM'er. I took him to the room where I had been sleeping on the floor with about 50 others and, seeing that he had nothing to sleep on, laid some padding and a blanket on the floor and used a towel for a pillow. He said it would be fine and he appreciated it very much.

As he was preparing for bed, I asked him if he had eaten. He had not as he had been travelling all day. I took him to the dining room but it was locked. So after picking the lock I found cornflakes, milk, bread, butter and jam—all of which he appreciated very much. As he ate, we began to fellowship. I asked where he was from. He said he and his wife had been working in Switzerland for several years in a ministry mainly to hippies and travelers. It was wonderful to talk with him and hear about his work and those who had come to Christ. When he finished eating, we turned in for the night.

However, the next day I was in trouble! The leaders of OM really "got on my case." "Don't you know who that man is on the floor next to you?" they asked. "It is Dr. Francis Schaeffer, the speaker for the conference!"

I did not know they were going to have a speaker, nor did I know who Francis Schaeffer was, nor did I know they had a special room prepared for him! After Francis Schaeffer became well known because of his books, and I had read more about him, I thought about this occasion many times—this gracious, kind, humble man of God sleeping on the floor with OM recruits! This was the kind of man I wanted to be.

Of course, I will never attain the intellect, knowledge or wisdom of Francis Schaeffer. But I can reach out to younger people and minister to them in Christ's name by living a life of humility. What about you?

Success is from God

The Lord *assigned* Paul and Apollos their roles, and growth is from God. The concepts of "assignment" and "growth" are crucial biblical teachings on success. Earlier, Paul asks the Corinthians, "What do you have that you did not receive?" (1 Cor. 4:7). John the Baptist counsels, "A person cannot receive even one thing unless it is given him from heaven" (John 3:27). James writes, "Every good gift and every perfect gift is from above, coming down from the Father of lights, with whom there is no variation or shadow due to change" (James 1:17). The key to contentment in relation to success and work is through working hard to please the Lord in your calling, and understanding there's no growth possible apart from him.

Your job: obedience. God's job: results.

God likes to use the weak to lead the strong because when the weak bear fruit, it's more obvious that God deserves the glory. Take me, for example. I didn't like school growing up. I played sports and thought those who read books were weird. I just hated reading and writing. Until I didn't.

Through a series of events in college, God placed in my heart a ravenous desire to read Christian books. Afterwards a desire to write emerged. If I'm used by God to touch lives through writing, it's not because I was a prodigious child destined to change the world. It's because the Lord likes to use unimpressive people to display his glory.

Working hard seems obvious. But how do you know what God has assigned you to do? In other words, how do you find your calling?

Contentment and Calling[17]

Your most important calling is your calling to Christ (Rom. 1:6; 1 Cor. 1:9). Regardless of who you marry, where you live, how many degrees you have, and how much money you make, the most significant reality of your life will always be that you are *in Christ*.

You don't just have one calling. You have multiple callings (yes, *callings*). Calling involves more than just work. Your calling is not just what you do for a living, but all of your roles in life and all of the tasks associated with those roles. Roles may include: mother, grandmother, citizen, father, pastor, neighbor, son, brother, writer, disciple, sister,

---

17.   I was immensely blessed by Dan Doriani's books on work entitled *Work* and *Work That Makes a Difference*.

friend, student, roommate, and so on. Whenever you are faithfully completing the tasks connected with your roles, you are fulfilling your calling.

Finding your calling is not a one-time spiritual decision you make about which degree to pursue or where to move, but about being faithful day in day out with all that God has entrusted to you. You don't have to find a calling; your callings find you as you obey God and serve others wherever God has placed you. And somehow, God gets you where he wants you to go as you obey him. You may plan your life, but God establishes your steps (Prov. 16:9).

Regarding work, a calling is ". . . work that flows from, expresses, and deepens our identity. A calling is our contribution to society, the labor that makes our lives matter. At best, it draws on our gifts and experiences and becomes our life's work, the task God prepared us to do."[18] This illustration provides guidance on finding a vocational calling:

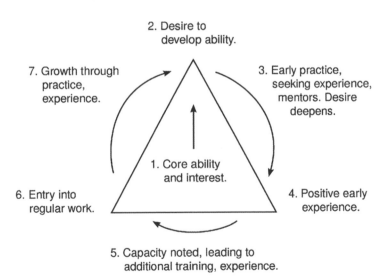

Figure 5.1. Finding a Calling from Dan Doriani, *Work, its Purpose, Dignity, and Transformation* (p. 98).

18.   Dan Doriani, *Work That Makes a Difference,* (Phillipsburg: P&R, 2021), 54.

As you pursue your vocational calling, consider the following:

Inward desires. Your desires, aspirations, and passions are not always trustworthy, but they shouldn't be ignored. God may place something on your heart he wants you to do (Neh. 7:5). Your desire to write or create music or start a business is not accidental. It may be a God-ordained means to help you discover your vocational calling.

External confirmation. Godly Christians are not easily swayed by uncritical admirers. External confirmation means honest feedback from trustworthy sources and a job offer in relation to your desires. Getting honest feedback is critical because we have blind spots and sometimes tend to have an overly inflated view of our abilities. Do other trusted sources who are doing what you want to do say you should do it too?

Character and motives. Ensure that you're embarking into your vocational choice for the right reasons. Without godly character you won't last for the long haul.

Opportunity. Doors must open, and you need lots of connections because connections are who usually open doors. Once I heard someone say, "Calling is confirmed by circumstances." Pay attention to how God is working through your circumstances. When God calls, he provides. If he hasn't provided, he's not calling—at least not yet. Trust his providential ability to create opportunities in his timing.

Needs. Seek to meet needs, remedy deficiencies, solve problems, and bear burdens.[19] If you seek personal fulfillment at work, you may not find it, but if you seek to meet needs through your work, fulfillment will find you.

Fulfill Your Calling

Although it's common to believe otherwise, there's no such thing as a secular/sacred divide in work. Some sectors of the Church believe only full-time ministry workers are serving God, but those who work "secular" jobs aren't. All honorable work, however, done for

---

19.   Dan Doriani, *Work*, 99.

the glory of God and good of neighbor is sacred. Although some work naturally lends itself to more influence, honest callings are morally equal.[20] You shouldn't feel "less than" if you are not in full-time vocational Christian ministry. You can glorify God as an accountant, teacher or entrepreneur. There is purpose in every respectable vocation.

As you work to fulfill your vocational calling, work at it with all your might. Don't compare yourself with others. If you do, you'll inevitably fall victim to either pride or envy; pride, because you are doing it bigger and better than someone else; or envy—or maybe even despair—because you notice many who are more fruitful than you. There's always going to be someone who is smarter and stronger and more attractive, but satisfaction comes when you work hard spending your time doing what God wants you to do, even if you never get a gold medal. Contentment is never found by comparing your life to others. Paul says to Timothy, "fulfil *your* ministry" (2 Tim. 4:5). Your ministry. Not someone else's.

Work in a fallen world brings "thorns and thistles" (Gen. 3:18). It's impossible to incessantly have 100 percent job satisfaction, even when fulfilling your calling. There will be failure, unemployment, financial difficulty, work overload, difficult bosses, and irritating co-workers. When times get hard at work, the temptation is to quit.

But don't—at least not right away.

You'll never experience contentment at work if you change vocations every two to three years. There needs to be a stickability about you. Even when turmoil arises, your knee-jerk reaction should be to endure, not to leave.[21] The way to endure difficulty with one of your callings is to remember that you are not there by accident, but God himself assigned you this calling and one day you will give an account to him for your labor. Feeling the weightiness of God

---

20.   Ibid, 87.
21.   Dan Doriani, *Work*, 102.

himself behind your calling helps you to pursue contentment, even under difficult circumstances.

You can change vocations, but when? Dan Doriani provides a three-worded formula: "Stay, unless, because."[22] He explains: "That is, stay where you are, unless there is reason to change, because of an overriding goal." Basically, stay unless you have justifiable reasons for doing so, like finding a new job that better suits your abilities, leaving your current role because you're being asked to sin or compromise your convictions, accepting a promotion to exercise more influence, or relocating to be closer to family. But quitting your job shouldn't be made lightly. You shouldn't change jobs for petty reasons. And even if you do find new work, there will be a list of aspects you don't like about *that* job once you get there. Hence, the necessity of contentment for long-term satisfaction regardless of where you work.

Probability of Success

Usually the way we talk about success is crass and incomplete. We think those who make it big do so because of talent, passion and work ethic. But life is never that simple. Everyone loves the outlandish rags to riches story about the guy who was born in the projects to a mom on drugs who mustered his way to a great college education and successful career through grit and determination. But even this person is the benefactor of unseen help. Only an insufferable egoist thinks they are self-made. Life in this world means ability does not always lead to achievement.

Major success is not something you manufacture. It's more of something you just so happened to walk into. I'm not saying work ethic, connections and shrewdness in your profession won't help you. They will. But when you examine factors that determine why one of two people with the same amount of talent have a disproportionate amount of influence, you'll see it's because of hundreds of uncontrollable factors. For unbelievers, this concept

---

22.   Ibid, 91. Based on 1 Corinthians 7.

is crushing because they are less in control of their lives than they think. For believers, however, this concept is liberating. It frees you to work hard and trust God with the results, knowing that God is sovereign over all hidden factors.

So what are these factors, anyway? This is the subject of Malcolm Gladwell's wildly entertaining book *Outliers: The Story of Success*, where Gladwell investigates the lives of highly successful people to understand the factors that contributed to their success. Success, according to Gladwell, is not the result of individual merit alone but the result of "accumulative advantages."[23] Advantages such as:[24]

1. **Family background and parenting.** What happens to you before you turn eighteen is massively important in determining how much success you will experience. For good or for ill, our parents shape us for life. Good, godly parenting can set you up for a lifetime of personal fruitfulness. Poor parenting can cause trauma and lifelong heartache without the possibility of fully recovering this side of eternity. The wealth and education levels of your parents and how involved they were in your life matter.

2. **Genetics.** I don't want to ruin your dreams, but genetics play a key role in some lines of work (like becoming a professional basketball player).

3. **Geographical location.** You cannot help but be shaped by where you come from and where you currently reside. Each geographical location provides a unique set of opportunities you can't get anywhere else. We tend to rise or fall based on the people with whom we associate and we don't always have the resources to relocate. There are cities in which the vibe, connections and opportunities are ripe for success, putting you at a severe disadvantage if you don't live there.

4. **The era in which you are born.** We are the product of the place and time in which we live. Our success is the direct result of the cultural factors that either propel or inhibit our success.

---

23. Malcolm Gladwell, *Outliers: The Story of Success* (New York: Back Bay Books, 2011), 30.

24. Some are from Gladwell; others are from personal observation.

5. **Opportunities.** This may be the biggest determinant of all. Success is directly related to: (1) the size and number of opportunities you get, (2) your ability to seize those opportunities, and (3) getting more, usually bigger and better, opportunities in light of your ability to seize the ones previously given. If you don't get any "big breaks," your influence will always remain small to medium-sized, no matter how hard you try. And in order to get big breaks, you often need connections with influential people.

My aim is twofold in sharing these factors. First, I'm trying to show you that you are not self-made. You are not the product of your own work ethic. You are the product of hundreds of people and thousands of factors that have enabled your success. Understanding that part of your success is generated by factors that you did not create promotes humility and encourages you to personally give thanks to mentors and coaches.

Second, the factors mentioned above shows the amount of success you experience is God's doing. Who is the one who determined your parents? Genes? The people who would be providentially placed around you? The place where you grew up? The era in which you were born? The opportunities you get? God. It is the hand of God behind all of these factors.

Work hard, make connections, be competent—but remember: ultimately, your life is in God's hands.

The Danger of Success[25]

Solomon says, "Do you see a man skillful in his work? He will stand before kings" (Prov. 22:29). Skill gets you attention, but there are burdens that accompany success that we don't realize until after we achieve it. Consider the very next chapter in Proverbs. After standing before kings because of skill, you may experience paranoia (23:1), indulgence (23:2), envy (23:3), overwork (23:4), and other issues that you would not have to deal with had you not stood before a king.

---

25. Burroughs, *Rare Jewel*, 103-109.

The blessings of success are not entirely positive. Too much success (especially at a young age) can ruin your life.

What are some negatives of success?

First, success is underwhelming. It's not as fulfilling as we had hoped. Ecclesiastes hints at this realization, but an insightful secular perspective is noted by cultural analyst David Brooks who, in his article *Five Lies our Culture Tells,* labels "career success is fulfilling" as one of them. Brooks writes:[26]

> This is the lie we foist on the young. In their tender years we put the most privileged of them inside a college admissions process that puts achievement and status anxiety at the center of their lives. That begins advertising's lifelong mantra—if you make it, life will be good. Everybody who has actually tasted success can tell you that's not true. I remember when the editor of my first book called to tell me it had made the best-seller list. It felt like … nothing. It was external to me. The truth is, success spares you from the shame you might experience if you feel yourself a failure, but career success alone does not provide positive peace or fulfillment. If you build your life around it, your ambitions will always race out in front of what you've achieved, leaving you anxious and dissatisfied.

Second, success creates burdens. Success reveals sinful aspects of your heart that you don't realize are there. Usually, more success means more spiritual warfare. Success increases the number of enemies (and frienemies) you'll have. More money and status usually lead to more pressure, stress and temptations. The rock star musician lives his dreams before thousands on the weekend but he may do drugs after the show to deal with personal emptiness. Burroughs says, "Many men and women look at the shine and glitter of prosperity, but they think little of the burden."[27]

Third, success increases temptation to pride. "If you have great success," Charles Spurgeon writes, "it will turn your head if

---

26. https://www.nytimes.com/2019/04/15/opinion/cultural-revolution-meritocracy.html

27. Burroughs, *Rare Jewel*, 103.

God does not permit you to be afflicted in some way or other."[28] Success has a way of undermining the help you received from God and others. Pride is the result. You start to take exclusive credit for accomplishments. You become self-reliant. How many pastors, for example, ceased private Bible study and prayer once their churches grew? Worse, success may make you think you are more loved by God than other Christians. After success, pride is close and humility is far away. God established a dynasty through King David that will never cease, but David's success in part led to sloth (2 Sam. 11:1), which in turn led to adultery and murder. Rare indeed is the person who walks away unscathed from a tremendous amount of success.

Fourth, success usually means more suffering. I am not aware of a single accomplished Christian who is not dealing with multiple pressing sorrows in private. God humbles his servants to keep them reliant on him. This is why A.W. Pink famously says, "It is doubtful whether God can bless a man greatly until he has hurt him deeply." The Apostle Paul is the most successful Christian ever, but he suffered an immeasurable amount of pain (2 Cor. 11:23-33).

Fifth, success increases responsibility. When God increases your success, he expects more from you (Luke 12:48). And so do other people.

Knowing that too much success creates unique temptations should encourage contentment. You really aren't missing out on much if you never become rich and famous. Don't envy the prosperous (Ps. 73:3). But also consider Romans 1:24: "Therefore God gave them up in the lusts of their hearts to impurity, to the dishonoring of their bodies among themselves . . ." The context is God's attitude and actions toward those who willingly suppress the truth of his existence. The words "God gave them up" are some of the scariest in Scripture. There's nothing worse than God giving up

---

28. Charles Spurgeon, *The Soul Winner*, (Fearn, Ross-Shire: Christian Focus Publications, 1992), 38-9.

on you. And what does that look like? Getting all that your heart desires (c.f. Rom 1:24; Rom. 1:26, Rom. 1:28), which may be more of a sign of God's curse than God's blessing.

Burroughs says the clearest sign to someone whom God does not intend to save is that God will give them over to their sinful desires:[29] "There is nothing that God conveys his wrath more through than a prosperous condition."[30] He adds, "The Lord conveys the plague of his curse through prosperity, as much as through anything in the world, and therefore when the soul comes to understand this, this makes it quiet and content."[31]

God's delay or denials of specific dreams may incline you to believe God is against you. The opposite is true. Tim Keller says that sometimes God seems to be killing us when he's actually saving us.[32] God expresses his fatherly love when he delays or denies some dreams. He knows too much success is not good for the human heart.

Seeking Success While Staying Content

Should you not pursue success? Perish the thought. We want to be as fruitful as possible with the means God has provided. I simply want to highlight the potential dangers of success. So we pray, "Lord, give me success, but not greater than my character!"[33]

In the world of work, contentment produces focus and security. I've never heard anyone at a job orientation say, "Contentment will make you successful at this company." But contentment is a prerequisite for long-term, Christ-honoring success in the workplace. Some people fear contentment will decrease productivity. But contentment fuels *long term* productivity. It's true that greed, impatience, and selfish ambition may make you more productive in the *short term,* but these sins will make you less productive in the long term because you'll either burn out or create character deficiencies or both. Contentment

---

29. Burroughs, *Rare Jewel,* 109.
30. Ibid, 109.
31. Ibid, 110.
32. Tim Keller, *Counterfeit Gods,* 20.
33. https://www.challies.com/christian-living/success-that-exceeds-sanctification/

ensures you won't be driven by fear or the unhealthy desire to be seen. It also ensures you won't regularly overwork because of selfish ambition or regularly underwork because of laziness.

As you seek success while pursuing contentment, keep the following in mind:

1. **Diligence**. Discover your abilities, talents and spiritual gifts, and serve diligently to produce high-quality work. Diligence is commended in Proverbs (Prov. 10:4; 12:14; 14:23), and hard work everywhere is encouraged in Scripture (1 Cor. 15:10). God prospered Hezekiah, but only after Hezekiah did his work "with all his heart" (2 Chron. 31:20-21). Work hard then pray, "Let the favor of the Lord our God be upon us, and establish the work of our hands upon us; yes, establish the work of our hands!" (Ps. 90:17).

2. **Network to serve.** Don't be a slick, back-slapping phony who clearly only wants to get something from others, but instead network to serve. Serve people without expecting anything in return. Good things tend to happen when you give your time and talents away without expectations. Many of the biggest opportunities I've had have come as a direct result of someone with power to open a door that I could not open for myself. Get good at building relationships and adding value. A wide social network creates opportunities and opportunities open doors for success.

3. **Work on your skills (and character).** If God inordinately grows your influence tomorrow, do you have the skills and character to handle it? It's easy to answer that question in the affirmative, but you can't say with certainty. Work on your craft and grow in godliness now, that way if God does promote you, you'll have the character to handle it.

4. **Trust God with the results.** Do everything in your power possible to manufacture success, then sleep well at night knowing the results are in God's hands.

Success: Unnecessary for Contentment

Nobody wants to be a failure, but you don't need success for personal happiness. Some of the most successful people in the world are also the most miserable. I find joy in life through enjoying God in my personal devotions, spending time with family and friends, enjoying God's creation in nature, getting a good night's sleep, drinking caffeine, reading and writing, watching sports and exercising. I can enjoy all of these on a regular basis without being known as successful. Instead of assuming that greater achievements will inevitably bring happiness, we should consider the activities in our lives that we love right now and make those activities a regular part of our day.

What do you enjoy doing? Photography? Gardening? Playing pickup volleyball? Be proactive about planning your days and weeks. Fill your calendar with activities that energize you. Most people who love the beach wished they lived by one. I live a mile away from the closest beach, and as I interact with others who likewise live by the beach, I'm amazed at how many people never go to the beach. Why? Lack of planning. They hurriedly tackle each day without any sense of control of their schedule, and months go by, and then they realize they haven't made time for their favorite activities. Pursuing contentment means taking action. In this case, take time each day or week to schedule your favorite activities.

God doesn't need you, but he is willing to use you. When Christ secured the salvation of God's people after dying on the cross and rising from the dead, he accomplished the most successful act in world history. Now we follow him as disciples knowing that we don't need to accomplish great achievements because his great achievement has already been accredited to you. As you walk closely with God, your desire for fruitfulness will surpass your desire for fame. The power of God can axe an unhealthy desire to be seen.

Jesus tells his disciples to rejoice that their names are written in heaven (Luke 10:20). If you are in Christ, your name is on the list and it will never be erased. If your name is written in heaven, you don't need your name written in lights. Success is not the goal of life, but to hear, "Well done, good and faithful servant" (Matt. 25:23).

Part 3

Cultivating Contentment

Chapter 7
Big God Thoughts

"For my own part, I tend to find the doctrinal books often more helpful
in devotion than the devotional books, and I rather suspect that the same
experience may await others. I believe that many who find that 'nothing
happens' when they sit down, or kneel down, to a book of devotion, would
find that the heart sings unbidden while they are working their way through a
tough bit of theology with a pipe in their teeth and a pencil in their hand."
— C.S. Lewis

Growing in contentment is not about one big life decision you make
on a Tuesday but rather the one hundred overlooked decisions you
make all week. You don't become content or discontent overnight.
Discontentment is a small drift; contentment is slowly accumulated.
You don't have to check your contentment temperature daily. Life
changes too frequently and progress happens too slowly to make a
daily spiritual check-in worthwhile.

As you pursue Christian contentment, you'll experience setbacks
and failures, and that's fine. Don't expect quick fixes. Growing
in contentment requires developing new habits of thinking and
feeling and doing, all of which take time. You won't have a bunch
of cheerleaders on your side. Most people have neither the care nor
concern to keep you accountable. Many of the decisions you'll have
to make to experience contentment will escape public eye. And
yet, by God's grace, progress in contentment is both attainable
and expected.

But how do you cultivate contentment?

You now understand a biblical view of contentment and how this
precious virtue applies to the big areas of your life. In this section,
you'll learn how to cultivate contentment.

Let's start with theology. Every Christian should seek increased knowledge of God. The deep things of God are not just for pastors but for all of God's people. Right knowledge of God leads to right thinking of God, which leads to right living for God and, consequently, contentment.

Let's examine the past, the path, and the plan.

The Past: The Rebellion and its Effects

Paradise, perfection. That's how I'd describe Adam and Eve's original circumstances in the Garden of Eden. But that state didn't last long.

In the beginning, God created the world from nothing, what theologians refer to as *ex nihilo,* and pronounced it "very good" (Gen. 1:31). This was a time of perfect shalom, which means "universal flourishing, wholeness, delight."[1] God desires to live with his creatures in shalom, but humans messed everything up in the third chapter of the Bible.

Sin didn't start with Adam and Eve. It started with Satan and his followers (Jude 6). Pride is likely the reason for the devil's fall (1 Tim. 3:6; Ezek. 28:11-19), which is why the wise man teaches pride comes before the fall (Prov. 16:18). The story of Adam and Eve's sinning in the Garden of Eden is often referred to as "the fall," but they didn't merely fall; they rebelled. The first human sin was a flat-out assault against a holy God.

In the Garden of Eden, Adam and Eve enjoyed perfect circumstances, and they were still not content. They wrongly thought sinning would make them happy. Humans still think this way. Original sin does not literally mean the first human sin committed, but the *effects* of Adam and Eve's sin on our world. Consider what their discontentment created. It led to pain and suffering, the fall of mankind, the beginning of every kind of sin, physical and spiritual death, and alienation from God and other people.

<hr />

1.   Cornelius Plantinga Jr., *Not the Way It's Supposed to Be: A Breviary of Sin* (Grand Rapids: Eerdmans, 1996), 10.

What is Sin?

Sin is wrongdoing in God's eyes. It means "Culpable disturbance of shalom."[2] It has the idea of missing the mark, not hitting the target, missing the goal, taking the wrong road. It's ". . . any act—any thought, desire, emotion, word, or deed—or its particular absence that displeases God and deserves blame."[3] It's not only the wrong actions you commit (commission) but also the right actions you're supposed to do but don't (omission). Sin is not restricted to actions, but also involves human desire and nature, and starts at birth: "Behold, I was brought forth in iniquity, and in sin did my mother conceive me" (Ps. 51:5). Sin is when people do right in their own eyes (Judg. 21:25).

Sin is the reason for most relational conflicts. Sin is why we age and ultimately die. It's the reason for misery, loneliness and death. It's the reason for youthful anxiety, midlife crises and regrets in old age. It's the reason for mental health issues, for sickness and disease, restlessness, shame, guilt, and meaninglessness. It's the reason why some leaders are passive and others are domineering. It's the reason for pain of giving birth, abusive men, and "thorns and thistles" (Gen. 3:18) from work, even work you love. Sin also has social, cultural and relational consequences. Consider King David. The illicit sex that David initiated with Bathsheba incurred God's judgment but also hurt Bathsheba, Uriah, Joab, David's army, and the entire nation of Israel. The more power and influence God entrusts to you, the more your sin hurts others. A holistic understanding of sin reveals why discontentment is so widespread.

After Adam and Eve's rebellion in the Garden of Eden, God quickly steps in and promises to send Jesus to make a way for sinful people to be right with God (Gen. 3:15), what theologians often refer to as the first announcement of the gospel. But the effects of the fall will be felt until Jesus comes back. We live in a sinful world ruled by the evil one (1 John 5:19), so it's irrational to expect

---

2. Ibid, 16.
3. Ibid, 13.

to have favorable circumstances at every turn in life. Because of the rebellion, our lives will simply never be what we desire on earth, and nobody is an exception to this rule. A robust doctrine of sin means you cannot possibly experience incessant satisfaction in this life, and you shouldn't expect to. Jesus is not a satisfaction genie.

It's important to understand the doctrine of sin because the more you do, the more you'll have realistic expectations for life in a fallen world. The doctrine of sin puts this life in its place. We are pilgrims on the way to our heavenly reward, not residents who have already arrived. If we ponder the consequences of sin and rejoice in our future heavenly existence, we'll be less confused by present earthly hardships and better equipped to live for the next life. If we remember that the New Creation is our permanent residence, and that through "many tribulations we must enter the kingdom of God" (Acts 14:22), then we'll realize that opposition, criticism, misunderstanding, sickness, relational conflict, financial difficulty, family drama, and spiritual warfare *are normal and expected aspects of ordinary Christian living.* You shouldn't be surprised if your life is hard. You *should* feel surprised if your life is a pain-free existence. Don't let our prosperous age fool you: technology and medical advances can't stop you from suffering.

The doctrine of sin teaches us how to think about contentment. When we suffer, we won't be surprised. When life goes well, we'll be incredibly thankful.

Confession and Contentment

God is both a loving father and a consuming fire (Heb. 12:29). Despite eternal acceptance received in Christ, growing in Christlikeness means growing in knowledge of your sin—and confessing and repenting quickly when made aware of it. You may find it helpful to follow the examples of the Puritans and regularly pray for forgiveness, even for unknown sins: "Lord, forgive me for my sins, known and unknown; confessed and unconfessed." Ongoing and unrepentant sin disrupts your fellowship with God, and God may withdraw a tangible sense of his presence as a way to invite you to repentance.

I understand pain and the temptations it creates. But sinning when you're in pain may at first provide relief, but it only will compound your problems. When I was in college, I felt like God was holding out on me. It felt like being a Christian was a killjoy because I couldn't engage in various sensual and drug-related activities that my secular friends boasted about. Then I watched my secular friends' lives. At first, they seemed to be having fun. And they were. But it didn't last long. One by one, I saw how their sin led to self-destruction. It took me several years to see that God wasn't holding out on me, but protecting me. God desires your flourishing, and flourishing comes through obeying him. Far from being an unwanted burden, the rules in Scripture are for your good. Ongoing sin makes you discontent because you were made for a life of flourishing through glorifying, enjoying and obeying God.

Remember What You Deserve

What's your biggest problem in life right now? Or what's the biggest problem you've ever had? Most people answer this question by pointing to undesired circumstances, like unwanted singleness, financial struggles or health issues. And these are real problems. I sure don't miss being single, I'm glad I'm saving for retirement, and the health issues I do have genuinely bother me. But your relationship status, money situation or health issues aren't your *biggest* problem. The biggest problem each person has is their sin in relation to God's holiness. This is why the gospel is so transferable in every culture—it relates to every person because every person is in need of a Savior. And if you are in Christ, your biggest problem has already been taken care of.

Some forms of modern Christian music often make a hard sell for what Jesus can do for you. The same is true for some evangelistic preaching. The messages sound like this: Are you broken and hurting? Are you filled with shame and guilt? Is your life a mess? Then turn it over to Jesus and let him clean you up. There are aspects to appreciate about these messages, but by and large, they are individualistic. It begins with man. It places man and his fulfillment at the center as opposed to God and his holiness. Our Christian message must start with God. The two questions each person must ask are: (1) Who is God, and (2) What does he command from me? As opposed to first seeing God as someone who could do something for you, you must see God as someone who you are accountable to.

When we first become Christians (especially true if you were converted in your adult years), we're overwhelmed by the grace of God. We are relieved that the deep longings of our soul have been fulfilled through knowing God and fulfilling our purpose on earth. We're so thankful to be saved that our lives are marked by gratitude and joy. We're quick to share the gospel with others. We feel overjoyed because of our right relationship with God. But as we go on into the Christian life, entitlement creeps in. Before we rejoiced in the joy of forgiveness, but now we complain when desires go unmet. In light of God's holiness, ponder again what your sins deserve: eternal condemnation, God's displeasure, and a life void of purpose and meaning. And yet, you have received eternal salvation, God's acceptance, and a life full of purpose and meaning. Your life may be hard, but you don't *deserve* a better life. Think deeply on what you deserve and rejoice in the benefits of salvation. You won't be happy with what you have until you understand what you deserve.

The joy of being reconciled to God and the hope of being in his presence for eternity provide enough joy to sustain you for a lifetime in this fallen world. When's the last time you rejoiced that your biggest problem in life has already been remedied?

The Path: Sanctification

Before the foundation of the world, God chose to adopt you. The moment you repented and trusted in Christ, God justified you forever. Apart from God opening your eyes to see the beauty of Jesus, you would have never become a believer. Salvation is 100 percent a work of the Lord.

But not sanctification. Sanctification is a dual effort.

What is sanctification? It's the glorious and messy process of God's power and your grace-driven effort to increasingly free you from sin and make you more holy. Simply stated, sanctification is the process of becoming more like Jesus.

Theologians differentiate between *definitive* sanctification and *progressive* sanctification. Definitive sanctification happens at conversion. When you trusted in Christ, God makes a *definitive* break from the world and sin in your life, permanently transferring you from darkness to light. God changed your desires (although not completely and fully) and started you on the lifelong path of becoming more like Jesus. It's a once and for all act. Sanctification is often discussed in terms of what you should do: read your Bible, pray, go to church. But not enough is said about what *God* does in your spiritual growth. God is more committed to your sanctification than you are.

Progressive sanctification, on the other hand, is God's power and your grace-driven effort to become more like Jesus. It's a dual effort. Consider Philippians 2:12-13: "Therefore, my beloved, as you have always obeyed, so now, not only as in my presence but much more in my absence, work out your own salvation with fear and trembling, for it is God who works in you, both to will and to work for his good pleasure." Notice Paul says work *out* your salvation, not work *for* your salvation. You work with all your might to grow in holiness, but God empowers the growth.

The phrase "make every effort" appears eight times in the New Testament. Each time the context is your effort in your spiritual growth. Change doesn't happen by accident. After telling us about his work ethic, Paul declares it's the grace of God that empowers him (1 Cor. 15:10). Exactly how your effort and God's power work together to make you like Christ is somewhat of a mystery. Although those who truly belong to Christ will inevitably become more like Christ, you have an active role to play in your Christian growth. Not for nothing did the Apostle Paul teach his audience to "present yourself to God" (Rom. 6:13; Rom. 12:1), to "flee from sexual immorality" (1 Cor. 6:18), and to "cleanse ourselves from every defilement of body and spirit" (2 Cor. 7:1). The author of Hebrews says to "strive" for peace and holiness (Heb. 12:14). Present, flee, and strive are not the work done by sluggards but by grace-driven Christians.

God's Plan for Your Life: Sanctification

Here's how contentment relates to sanctification. Christians often wonder about God's personal plan for their lives. Should I marry that person? Go to that college? Move to that city? Good questions. We can't know all the future details of our lives, but we know what's in Scripture, and Scripture teaches that God's Plan A for your life is your sanctification: "For this is the will of God, your sanctification: . . ." (1 Thess. 4:3).

God saved you to be holy (1 Pet. 1:15-16; Rom. 6:19). Holiness is a big deal to God. It should also be a big deal to you. Holiness is not the basis of salvation, but it is the evidence of it. The Reformers used to say that we're saved by faith alone but that faith is never alone. When we struggle with discontent, we usually have turned our eyes away from Christlikeness and onto our present circumstances. Focus on walking faithfully with God, day in day out, not fretting over the future details in your life. And when the storms and setbacks arrive, continue walking faithfully knowing that, even though you don't have a clue what God is doing, God knows what he's doing, and he's making you more like Jesus.

If God's Plan A is to make you more like Jesus, you shouldn't be surprised when you suffer, because the Suffering Servant was known as "a man of sorrows" (Isa. 53:3). The ideal Western life—a spouse, 2.5 kids, a white picket fence, and a life of success and comfort—is incompatible with the call to take up your cross and follow Jesus. Far from being a life of misery, holiness is the pathway to true happiness. Your role in this fallen world is better understood and appreciated by focusing on obeying God rather than trying to create and perfect a man-made five-year vision plan.

126

When we remember that God makes no mistakes and uses all of our pain to make us more like Jesus, and that God has a specific reason for the heartbreaks and setbacks, we can rejoice and cultivate contentment (Phil. 1:29; James 1:2-4). We can cease holding too tightly to our dreams or money or a relationship. We focus less on what we obtain and more on who we become.

Understanding God's aim for your life provides spiritual stability and deep contentment amidst the ups and downs of life. May we never become so theologically astute that we roll our eyes at Romans 8:28: "for those who love God all things work together for good."

I love how Martin Luther puts it:

> This life therefore is not righteousness, but growth in righteousness, not health, but healing, not being but becoming, not rest but exercise. We are not yet what we shall be, but we are growing toward it, the process is not yet finished, but it is going on, this is not the end, but it is the road. All does not yet gleam in glory, but all is being purified.

The Plan: Providence

An unshakeable faith in God's providence is essential for Christian contentment, so much so that one author includes providence in his definition of contentment: "Contentment is the inward, gracious, quiet spirit that joyfully rests in God's providence."[4]

But what is providence?

Sovereignty + Goodness = Providence

The original Latin word from which we get the word *providence* means "to see beforehand, a prior seeing, a foresight." Providence is about God's ongoing involvement with the world. It combines two of God's attributes: sovereignty and goodness. Sovereignty is God's right and power to do what he wills.[5] Goodness, on the other hand, displays God's excellence, beauty, perfection, and skill in all

---

4. Erik Raymond, *Chasing Contentment: Trusting God in a Discontented Age* (Wheaton: Crossway, 2017), 23.
5. This is roughly how John Piper puts it.

his activity. Goodness shows God's "benevolence."[6] God's goodness means everything he sends in your life is for your benefit. So a layman's definition for providence may sound like this: God controls all events in your life to fulfill a specific purpose he has for you in such a way that demonstrates his sovereignty and goodness. John Piper defines providence in two words: "purposeful sovereignty."[7]

One Confession puts it this way[8]:

> God the great Creator of all things doth uphold, direct, dispose, and govern all creatures, actions, and things, from the greatest even to the least, by his most wise and holy providence, according to his infallible foreknowledge, and the free and immutable counsel of his own will, to the praise of the glory of his wisdom, power, justice, goodness, and mercy.

The Heidelberg catechism speaks of God's providence as "all things come not by chance, but by his fatherly hand." The Belgic Confession speaks of God's control over all events "in such a way that nothing happens in this world without God's orderly arrangement." I love the expressions "Fatherly hand" and "orderly arrangement." It reminds us of God's intentional administration of our lives. God's involvement in your life is not mechanical, but purposeful, intentional and personal.[9] Of course, God's providence doesn't minimize our responsibility in making God-honoring decisions, but it does provide the comfort of knowing God's hand is behind all of our decisions. Providence means there's no such thing as chance, randomness, karma, or luck, and there is never need for paranoia or superstition. It provides tremendous peace and joy during uncertain times and changing circumstances.

---

6. John Frame, *The Doctrine of God* (Phillipsburg: P&R Publishing, 2002), 402-10.
7. John Piper, *Providence* (Wheaton: Crossway, 2021), 29.
8. Westminster Confession of Faith, 5.1
9. John Frame, *The Doctrine of God*, 276.

Providence and Your Life

Providence means God is with you every step of the way, always demonstrating his power and goodness in your life. Obstacles, setbacks, failures, and disappointments do not hinder God's plan for you; they *are* God's plan for you. In these moments we lament and confess that we don't fully understand each detail of our present circumstances, but God's providence provides inward spiritual stability to continue to walk in trust. We lay our heads on our bedroom pillow in peace, knowing all the details of the day were under God's control. And as you reflect on your life, then and only then will you be able to better trace God's hand. As one Puritan says, "The providence of God is like a Hebrew word—it can only be read backwards!"[10]

When you deeply consider God's involvement in your life, you cannot help but utter praise and thanks. It gives you reason to bless the Lord always. It promotes thankfulness in all circumstances (1 Thess. 5:18). It removes superstitious activity and kills the need for OCD behavior. If God prospers us, we know it's for our personal enjoyment and to bless others. When we suffer, we know it's for our good. So providence kills the pride that says we deserve better, and it kills the despair that falsely believes God has deserted us. Providence commands worship.

Painting and Providence

Bob Ross was a famous painter from the twentieth century whose TV show *The Joy of Painting* was a major hit, capturing the hearts of millions. I'm not a big arts guy, but I think his paintings are captivating. They are spectacular—but they never start that way. When I watch Bob start a painting, I think, "What in the world are you doing?" He seems to irresponsibly smack those oil paints on the canvas. As he begins his painting, I have no idea where he is going or how in the world he's going to turn that smack of paint on the canvas into a beautiful masterpiece. But slowly but surely, he does. As Bob

---

10. Quoted in John Frame, *The Doctrine of God*, 286.

paints, a masterpiece is steadily revealed, and I begin to marvel. I'm totally hooked and then mesmerized at the end by how he was able to turn what started with globs of oil paint into a beautiful painting.

Such is the case with our lives and God's providence. Your life story is being written by a perfect author. Don't think robotic machinery. Our lives, instead, are like a painting, a sculpture, a drama, a movie, a novel.[11] We are not promised a beautiful ending in this life, but we are promised that God's purposes will prevail as we obey him.

---

11. John Piper, *Providence*, 19.

Chapter 8
Eight Rules for Contentment

"People do not drift toward holiness. Apart from grace-driven effort, people do not gravitate toward godliness, prayer, obedience to Scripture, faith, and delight in the Lord. We drift toward compromise and call it tolerance; we drift toward disobedience and call it freedom; we drift toward superstition and call it faith. We cherish the indiscipline of lost self-control and call it relaxation; we slouch toward prayerlessness and delude ourselves into thinking we have escaped legalism; we slide toward godlessness and convince ourselves we have been liberated." — D.A. Carson

Edward Bouverie Pusey was an English scholar, theologian, and preacher from the 1800s, who served as a leader in the Oxford church movement as a professor of Hebrew at Oxford University. His "five rules for contentment" are both simple and profound. "If we wished to gain contentment," he writes, "we might try such rules as these:"

Rule #1: Allow thyself to complain of nothing, not even of the weather.

Rule #2: Never picture thyself to thyself under any circumstances in which thou art not.

Rule #3: Never compare thine own lot with that of another.

Rule #4: Never allow thyself to dwell on the wish that this or that had been, or were, otherwise than it was, or is. God Almighty loves thee better and more wisely than thou dost thyself.

Rule #5: Never dwell on the morrow. Remember that it is God's, not thine. The heaviest part of sorrow often is to look forward to it. 'The Lord will provide.'[1]

---

1. Quoted in Melissa Kruger, *Contentment*, (Sanford, FL: Ligonier Ministries, 2018), CD.

You may think these rules are over-spiritualized. Or you may think these rules are forgotten treasures of church history. Either way, rules like these reinforce the idea that learning contentment isn't always about deep teaching. Sometimes, it's a one-liner that changes your life. That's what this chapter is all about.

Eight More Rules for Contentment

How do we picture someone who is content? Usually what comes to mind is a person lying in a hammock by a pool on a nice summer day with the breeze running through their hair and a drink in their hand. They are in and out of sleep consciousness. When awake, they sip their drink every ten minutes while saying, "Ahh." All that was required to experience inward peace and satisfaction was to lay in a hammock by a pool on a sunny day.[2]

But . . . no.

That's not how contentment works. Growing in contentment requires effort. The psalmist says, "Unless the Lord builds the house, those who build it labor in vain" (Ps. 127:1). Without the Lord's blessing, we labor in vain, but notice: the laborers still have to build. As J.I. Packer says in one book endorsement, "The Christian's motto should not be 'Let go and let God' but 'Trust God and get going.'"

Here are some rules to get you going.

Rule #1: Take Action

There's always something, isn't there? Life is a series of trials, one after another. You get sick after coming home from vacation. Shortly after recovering from your sickness, you get a flat tire while driving home from work. After leaving the mechanic, you hear bad news from a family member. After recovering from the initial shock of the bad news, you get laid off from your job. After finding a new job, you realize you don't like your boss. After a bad performance review, you learn your best friend is moving to a new city. In search of new friends, you sign up for sand volleyball, only to sprain your ankle during the second game of the season. It never ends!

---

2. I'm thankful to Melissa Kruger for this illustration.

The reason the church emphasizes Christian contentment is to help God's people cope with the conveyor belt of trials and changing circumstances. The harsh reality of living in a fallen world means that you cannot obtain perfect circumstances in this life. Even ideal circumstances don't last long. Hence, expressions like, "True Christian contentment is not found in your circumstances, but in Christ. Seek contentment in Christ, not your circumstances." True. And although there is nothing you can do about *some* of your unfavorable circumstances, that is not true about *all* of your circumstances. Don't like your circumstances? Then do something about it.

You are not in this season of life by accident. God's invisible hand has guided you with each decision and step you have made. God's guidance in your life provides a remarkable amount of comfort since God is both good and wise. But as we've seen, God's sovereignty doesn't mitigate human responsibility. So if you don't like your present circumstances, ask, "Are there any God-approved steps I can take today to change them?"

Consider pain areas of your life where discontent abounds and make a list of what action steps you can take today to help. Here are some examples:

- **Loneliness.** Text one person in my church to hang out with every week. I will seek friendships as opposed to waiting for them to come to me.
- **Personal health:** Learn how to cook two healthy new recipes. Sign up for a gym membership and commit to going three times per week.
- **Unwanted singleness:** Seek wise counsel from older, trusted and mature married Christians, then consider signing up for an online dating site.

Pray, "God, help me to be content" and then answer your own prayer by taking wise action. All I'm saying is that there are probably steps that you can take today to move toward contentment but you have neglected to take them because you believe you are powerless to help create any change in your life. The practical (what you do) and spiritual (what God does) go together. Christians often divorce the practical from the spiritual, but they're interconnected.

Rule #2: Count God's Mercies[3]

I read the story about a man who went to a minister for counseling. He was in the midst of a financial collapse.

"I've lost everything," he bemoaned.

"Oh, I'm so sorry to hear that you've lost your faith."

"No," the man corrected him, "I haven't lost my faith."

"Well, then I'm sad to hear that you've lost your character."

"I didn't say that," he corrected, "I still have my character."

"I'm sorry to hear that you've lost your salvation."

"That's not what I said," the man objected, "I haven't lost my salvation."

"You have your faith, your character, your salvation. Seems to me," the minister observed, "that you've lost none of the things that really matter."[4]

Losing temporal things does hurt. But having an eternal perspective helps you to deal with loss. Having the right perspective in life is crucial for personal contentment, and feelings of gratitude and acts of thankfulness help provide this perspective. In fact, thankfulness is part of God's will for your life: ". . . give thanks in all circumstances; for this is the will of God in Christ Jesus for you" (1 Thess. 5:18). You can always be sure that you are in the revealed will of God when you are thanking him. Arguably, the most practical way to grow in Christian contentment is through giving genuine and heartfelt thanks to God. Being thankful isn't a natural response for anyone, and those who consider themselves thankful usually underestimate how often they actually give thanks to God. Thankfulness starts with an inward gratitude toward God, yes, but it cannot end there. In order to express biblical thanks, you must

3.   Burroughs, *The Rare Jewel of Christian Contentment*, 171.
4.   http://firstbaptistrockville.org/sermon/things-that-really-matter/

thank God with your words either audibly (or silently) in extended (or short) prayers of thanks. Thankfulness is not complete until it is expressed with words.

By practicing gratitude, we mirror the psalmists who were aware of God's blessings (Ps. 40:5). Pay attention to how God is working in your life right now and be deliberate about tracking your mercies. Counting money requires thoughtfulness, and so too does counting God's blessings. Thankfulness is simple, so we assume it's easy. But it's not. Just because something is simple doesn't mean it's easy. Growing in thankfulness requires work. But, over time, the cumulative effect of intentional thankfulness will bear significant fruit. The world loves spontaneity and novelty, but Christian growth comes through ancient, mundane and oft-overlooked habits like gratitude.

Thankfulness is not limited to the big blessings of life. We must be thankful for the little blessings, too. Seen this way, Christian thankfulness is done on a macro (the big stuff) and a micro (the small stuff) level. You will never learn thankfulness if you can't thank God for ice and sunshine and a chair to sit on. These seem like trite blessings, but many Christians in the world don't have them, and many Christians in previous generations never did. How unbelievably spoiled we are when we cannot recognize God's goodness in the small blessings of life. Be on the lookout for mercies and express thanks. You may decide to add structure to help you be intentional. Some ideas:

1. **Keep a contentment journal.** Write down God's mercies. Just one to three blessings per day or week is a good start.

2. **Thank God in prayer.** I often rush into supplication and neglect thankfulness, or I thank God at the end of my prayer time after going through my list. God is our Father, and it is good and right to ask for material gifts. But we forfeit much joy in our lives simply because we don't spend enough time thanking God in prayer.

3. **Be silently thankful throughout your day.** Prayer doesn't always have to be a long, drawn-out, audible exercise (although

it sometimes should be). Like Nehemiah (Neh. 2:4), we can utter quick prayers. You create a heightened spiritual awareness of God's presence when you are deliberate about thanking him silently in your mind throughout your day.

Pens have eyes.[5] What you see has a direct correlation to your levels of contentment: "For all that is in the world—the desires of the flesh and the desires of the eyes and pride of life—is not from the Father but is from the world" (1 John 2:16). Putting Netflix, magazines and social media before your eyes all day is asking for misery. Putting God's blessings before your eyes cultivates contentment. Writing down blessings you're grateful for is more powerful than merely thinking about it.

If you feel discontent, write down a list of things you're grateful for. Or maybe write down a list of things you deserve or don't deserve.[6] If you're having relational conflict with someone right now, write down three things for which you are thankful about that person. Either way, don't just ponder; write it down.

A 2003 study published in the *Journal of Personality and Social Psychology* reveals that people who feel gratitude don't get sick as often, have better immune systems, and report fewer aches and pains. They also experience more positive emotions, sleep better, and have better social lives.[7] Secular people are motivated to be thankful in order to experience one less fever. And that's fine. But as disciples of Christ, we have a million more reasons to be thankful. We have been chosen by God before the world began, engrafted into his people, saved from his wrath, experienced the forgiveness of all sins, given the perfect righteousness of Christ, and now experience union with him. This glorious salvation that we have received through Christ, and all the blessings associated with it, should be cause for

---

5.   I got this idea from John Piper.
6.   Erik Raymond, *Chasing Contentment*, 62.
7.   Quoted in Amy Morin, *13 Things Mentally Strong People Don't Do: Take Back Your Power, Embrace Change, Face Your Fears, and Train your Brain for Happiness and Success* (New York: William Morrow Paperbacks, 2017), 31.

unending praise to our Lord, as articulated in question two of the Heidelberg Catechism:

Q. What must you know to live and die in the joy of this comfort?

A. Three things: first, how great my sin and misery are; second, how I am set free from all my sins and misery; third, *how I am to thank God for such deliverance* (emphasis added).

Evergreen trees, unlike most trees, are green all year round. Summer heat, green. Crisp fall, green. Spring rain, green. Freezing winter and, once again, green. No matter the weather, evergreen trees are green. Something similar could be said about God's people in relation to personal thankfulness: no matter your current circumstances, be thankful because God is always worthy of thanks.

Rule #3: Guard Your Heart

Buddhism teaches that suffering results from desire. If your desires cease, so will your pain. Get to this point, and you've reached Nirvana, a state which doesn't mean utopia on earth, but nothingness. Nirvana is the ultimate goal of Buddhism. Buddhism, of course, is a heretical religion that fails to see that humans are created in the image of the God of the Bible, and as image bearers, we should not aim to end our desires, but to redirect them. This redirection is done through your heart.

The "heart" in the Bible is not the physical organ that pumps blood to the rest of your body but is a metaphor which describes the center of your being: thoughts, desires, feelings, intellect. Your heart is not just the seat of your emotions. Your heart is who you are at your core. Ultimately, your heart determines all that you do and say (Luke 6:45). And although some people may try to separate their thinking from their feeling, what you think and feel are interconnected.

Our actions always follow our strongest desires. In order to change and grow in contentment, we must change how we think, what we desire and, ultimately, what we worship. Worship is not limited to the four songs we sing on Sunday but encompasses all of life. For your desires to change, your heart must be continually transformed and directed toward God. As the saying goes, the heart of the matter is the matter of the heart.[8]

The world says, "Follow your heart." It means do whatever you desire. The follow your heart mantra is the fruit of individualism which attempts to replace God with self. You should not always follow your heart because sometimes your heart desires sin. God loves you too much to always give you what your heart desires. Instead of blissfully following your heart, you should redirect your heart toward the ways of truth: "Hear, my son, and be wise, and direct your heart in the way" (Prov. 23:19).

Two biblical passages on the heart have always struck me. Proverbs 4:23 is the first one: "Keep your heart with all vigilance, for from it flow the springs of life." The call is to "keep your heart" (ESV), or "Watch over your heart" (NASB). The NIV is stronger: "Above all else, guard your heart." Bruce Waltke says, ". . . it [your heart] must be reckoned as more important than anything else that one needs to restrain."[9] In this passage, a parent is giving his son advice about living wisely. Just a few verses earlier the father tells his son to pay close attention to his appeal (v.20), and to keep his father's words (v.21). The father is passing down nuggets of wisdom and then gives his best advice: guard your heart. This is an essential biblical teaching. "Guard your heart" is not some touchy-feely slogan to put on a bumper sticker but is a matter of life or death, salvation or destruction, growth or failure.

This language is strong. It's alarming to give a list of important ideas and then say, "Above all else . . ." Such is the enthusiasm the teacher of wisdom gives about guarding your heart. We say to pastors, "Above all else, guard your study time." To singles, "Above all else, don't marry a non-Christian." To gatekeepers, "Above all else, don't fall asleep." When we say "above all else" and then give a

---

8.   I was aided by Wayne Grudem's sermon "Keep Your Heart with All Vigilance." https://www.youtube.com/watch?v=biUvG1GkWgA

9.   Bruce K. Waltke, *The Book of Proverbs: Chapters 1-15* (Grand Rapids: Eerdmans, 2004), 297.

crucial action item to obey, we're not saying there aren't other things you can and should be doing on top of that one thing. But we are saying that what follows after "above all else" is the most important step to achieving your goal. Above all else, to acquire wisdom you must guard your heart.

How do you guard yours? Guarding your heart means keeping a close watch on it, keeping it in check and protecting it from evil.[10] It means being careful about the information you consume. Seen this way, guarding your heart has both offensive and defensive components. On the offensive side, guarding your heart means to abide in Christ, which brings me to the second passage on the heart that sticks out to me: "Delight yourself in the LORD, and he will give you the desires of your heart" (Ps. 37:4). This verse does not teach that if you delight yourself in the Lord, the Lord will then give you all of the desires you presently have, but that as you delight yourself in the Lord, the Lord's desires and yours will coincide. When you seek the Lord in private and devote yourself to your local church, you are redirecting your heart toward the ways of God. Guarding your heart from the offensive side means doing activities that will help your emotions, feelings, thoughts and all aspects of your inner well-being.

On the defensive side (and probably more importantly), guarding your heart means avoiding activities that will hurt your emotions, feelings, thoughts and all aspects of inner well-being. It means avoiding relationships with those who desire to sin. It looks like a goalie in hockey who stays alert and strategically positions himself to prevent the opposing team from scoring. Lots of social media use and low Scripture intake, for example, reveals a careless disposition about guarding your heart. You're not playing defense well; you're letting the other team score effortlessly. Consume content that will help your heart; get rid of all of the stuff that's hurting you. Much of growing in contentment is learning how to obey Proverbs 4:23.

---

10.   Ibid, 297.

To determine if your desires are in line with God's Word, here are three questions to ask:

1. Do I have a longing for something I could never reasonably hope to acquire in a morally right way?
2. Has God given me the ability to fulfill this desire?
3. Can I take God-approved actions to begin to move toward attaining what I desire or must I sin to obtain it?[11]

Having desires is part of what it means to be created in the image of God, but if you are willing to sin to *fulfill* a desire or if you sin *in response* to unfulfilled desires, then you are struggling with discontentment. When desires become demands, discontentment is near.[12]

Desires must be trained, controlled and submitted to God. We live in an expressive individualistic age where desires eclipse everything. But the Christian life is not about expressing yourself, but dying to yourself (Matt. 16:24). We get life by dying.

The world says that you can be anything you want to be and have anything you want to have as long as you work hard and put your mind to it, but the world is wrong. Life in a fallen world means that every person without exception dies with some unfulfilled dreams. Although living with unfulfilled dreams is painful, we know we're heading for the New Creation where we'll never experience longing again.

Rule #4: Prioritize Faithful Local Church Involvement and the Spiritual Disciplines

The God of the Bible—Father, Son, and Holy Spirit—lives in community as one God in three persons, providing the basis for his people to likewise live in community. Private Bible reading and prayer are essential for Christian contentment, but not sufficient. You are commanded by God to gather for corporate worship (Heb. 10:25). There can hardly be Christian growth without a

---

11. Wayne Grudem, *Christian Ethics*, 1175-1776.
12. Dave Harvey, *Rescuing Ambition*, 120.

devotion to the local church. Christianity is not "Me and Jesus," but rather "My God and my church."

The local church is the heart of Christian discipleship. God works to grow your faith when you gather with God's people in a way that he does not work as you follow your personal Bible reading plan. Something happens at a deep, subconscious level—often in a way we cannot articulate but can undoubtedly feel—when God's people gather in corporate worship. As you join your church to sing, pray, fellowship, confess sin, receive communion, and hear the Word of God preached, you're becoming deeply formed in Christ. As you prioritize local church involvement, you'll care less about earthly issues and will care more about playing your part in the great commission.

Growth happens best in community. You need to bear burdens and cast them (Gal. 6:1-5). You need wise counsel to reveal blind spots and trusted Christians to imitate (and rebuke you when necessary). Although friendships can be frustrating, hurtful and time-consuming, withdrawing from community is a form of self-absorption (Prov. 18:1) that will worsen your discontent. Unless providentially hindered, join your church for public worship whether you feel like it or not. Regular church attendance is not a matter of personal preference but a matter of spiritual life or death. You cannot experience long-term contentment without making the church a non-negotiable priority. I've never admired the spiritual life of a professing Christian who regularly skips corporate worship.

But what about Monday through Saturday?

Few books have edified my devotional life more than George Müller's autobiography. Müller is famous in part for his prayer life. He started and funded an orphanage not through financial support letters but through prayer alone. Müller once famously said:

> I saw more clearly than ever, that the first great and primary business to which I ought to attend every day was, to have my soul happy in the Lord. The first thing to be concerned about was not, how much I might serve the Lord, how I might glorify the Lord;

but how I might get my soul into a happy state, and how my inner man may be nourished. . . I saw that the most important thing I had to do was to give myself to the reading of the Word of God and to meditate on it.

Jesus tells us that apart from him we can do nothing (John 15:5). Nothing means . . . nothing. You can look that word up in Greek and Hebrew and it means the same thing. We are utterly dependent on God for life and breath and growth and everything. Having spent an hour or two with our church family on Sunday (or whichever day you meet), Christians now spend intentional time with the God they love throughout the week. Like Müller, we must get our souls happy in the Lord through the spiritual disciplines, especially unhurried Bible reading and prayer.

God does the heavy lifting in your personal sanctification, but part of what it means to "work out your own salvation with fear and trembling" (Phil. 2:12) is to grow in Christlikeness through grace-driven effort. We are justified by grace alone, but as you seek growth in godliness, remember that "grace" and "effort" are not enemies. It is a delight to exert effort to become more like Christ. Like all relationships, the strength of your walk with God will partly depend on how much time and effort you put into it.

For you, maybe it's early morning before your spouse and kids wake up. Or it might be during your lunch break or before bed. It doesn't have to be long, and it doesn't have to look like everyone else's devotional life, but if we are going to grow in contentment, we need to be regularly connecting with God.

Rule #5: Practice Bodily Stewardship

Long before I became a pastor, I was a certified specialist in sports nutrition medicine and personal training. I spent a couple of years studying and working in the field of supplements, exercise and nutrition. Sometimes doing practical things like taking a nap reaps wonders for your spiritual life. Contentment is easier to experience when you take good care of your body.

D.A. Carson agrees:

> If you keep burning the candle at both ends, sooner or later you will indulge in more and more mean cynicism—and the line between cynicism and doubt is a very thin one. Of course, different individuals require different numbers of hours of sleep; moreover, some cope with a bit of tiredness better than others. Nevertheless, if you are among those who become nasty, cynical, or even full of doubt when you are missing your sleep, you are morally obligated to try to get the sleep you need. We are whole, complicated beings: our physical existence is tied up to our spiritual well-being, to our mental outlook, to our relationships with others, including our relationship with God. Sometimes the godliest thing you can do in the universe is get a good night's sleep—not pray all night, but sleep. I'm certainly not denying that there may be a place for praying all night; I'm merely insisting that in the normal course of things, spiritual discipline obligates you to get the sleep your body needs.[13]

Take care of your body. Consume supplements (e.g. vitamins, minerals, protein powder, etc.) Drink lots of water. Exercise three to five days a week. Get adequate sleep at night, even if that means nine hours. You're not being lazy. You're practicing bodily stewardship. Practicing self-care is not selfish. If you're not taking care of yourself, you won't be much good for others.

Enjoy your cheat meals and favorite beverages, but know that what you put in your body will have a direct correlation to how you feel. You may have health issues or chronic pain, but do your best to practice bodily stewardship with the body you have.

But there's more.

Rest is not just physical. You can get eight hours of sleep at night but still feel exhausted. Rest is also emotional, mental, spiritual and scenic. Here are examples on how to rejuvenate for each:

- **Emotional:** Surround yourself with people who energize you. Consider ending toxic relationships. Continue to love difficult

---

13. D. A. Carson, *Scandalous: The Cross and the Resurrection of Jesus* (Wheaton: Crossway, 2010), 147.

people, but place boundaries when necessary. Regularly express your concerns and feelings with trusted Christian friends.

- **Mental:** Don't use technology at least one day a week.
- **Spiritual:** Connect with God daily.
- **Scenic:** Take a vacation or a getaway. Get outside and enjoy nature often.

Taking care of your body means rest beyond daily sleep. It means practicing the Sabbath (Ex. 20:8-11). Work five or six days a week, then completely take one day off. A weekly day off sounds like torture for over-achievers, but when you rest from work one day a week, you demonstrate that you trust God for provision and work is not your identity. There's more to life than spreadsheets and sales calls. Honoring the fourth commandment provides more energy for the long haul. You don't need a PhD in Old Testament to see the benefits of taking one day a week off from work, you will be a better employee if you do.

You also need silence and solitude, a lesson I learned the hard way when we moved into a home near our church. The problem? We overlooked the fact that the house was near the highway and we could hear the vehicles in our home as if they were right there in the house. Noise may increase stress levels. On a regular basis, you need time away from noise to think, pray, read and just be. You need getaways and vacations. Take all of your allotted vacation time and don't feel guilty about it. We are not only called to steward creation but also to enjoy it.

Rule #6: Stay Productive and Work Hard

C.S. Lewis writes:

> We are always falling in love or quarreling, looking for jobs or fearing to lose them, getting ill and recovering, following public affairs. If we let ourselves, we shall always be waiting for some distraction or other to end before we can really get down to our work. The only people who achieve much are those who want

knowledge so badly that they seek it while the conditions are still unfavorable. Favorable conditions never come.[14]

They never do, at least not in this life. That means we need to continue being faithful in our callings until the Lord promotes us to glory. Instead of seeking distractions every two seconds to relieve nagging feelings of emptiness, we should stay productive and work hard at what God has called us to do, knowing that fulfillment sometimes rewards the faithful and appropriately busy.

Rule #5 is to practice bodily stewardship, which entails rest. Now I'm talking about hard work. Contradiction? No. Paradox. We need not separate the two: when it's time to work, work hard; when it's time to rest, unwind completely. They go together. Working hard increases your appreciation of rest.

In his book, *Flow: The Psychology of Optimal Experience,* psychologist Mihaly Csikszentmihalyi says that people are happiest when they are in a state called *flow,* the feeling of complete engagement in work. The work must be challenging but doable. It's when you lose track of time and experience personal enjoyment because you are immersed in a task, whether there is monetary gain or not. Flow makes the sorrows of life feel more manageable and makes us less prone to check Instagram or email every twenty minutes. Regardless of your annual income, if you set goals and work hard at doing what you love, you tend to feel happier.

It's become popular in recent years for Christians to write against busyness, and surely good has come from some of these writings. But don't forget the Bible rebukes idleness (2 Thess. 3:11) and laziness. Being too busy all the time is bad for obvious reasons, but God created humans to work and work hard. Often, the deeply rooted issues behind our personal fatigue are not busyness, but distraction (because we are addicted to social media), fear of man (because we can't say "no"), and the quest for significance (trying to justify our existence through accomplishments).

---

14. C.S. Lewis, *The Weight of Glory* (New York: HarperOne, 2001), 60.

Consider Jesus. The word "immediately" appears over forty times in the Gospel of Mark. Clearly, Jesus was no idle man. He was busy serving others, doing the work the Father gave him—securing the salvation of God's people through his perfect life, death and resurrection. Jesus was busy. No, he was not incessantly busy. The Gospels often mention his rising early to pray and escape the crowds. But his life was not characterized by inactivity.

Not for a second am I saying you should say "yes" to every request. You might need more margin in your life. But most of us are less busy than we think. "I'm busy" is how we respond when people ask how we're doing because it's culturally acceptable, but our days are filled with an inordinate amount of time on social media and entertainment. Many of us wish we had more time, but a better remedy is to grow in time management and self-discipline. Staying busy and working hard (and working smart) to provide value in your calling helps fight discontentment because when you are intentional about staying busy and working hard, you don't have time to sit around and feel self-pity.

I also encourage you to celebrate your victories. Once you reach a milestone in life, do something to commemorate it. Life is filled with so many sorrows that, once you accomplish one of your goals, you should take time to celebrate. Weddings today are less than an hour, but in Jesus' day you needed to block out an entire week or so for partying if you said "yes" on your RSVP. If you don't celebrate your successes, then you'll never *feel* successful because you'll just frantically rush on to the next goal and then wonder, "Am I accomplishing anything with my life?" Eating at your favorite restaurant to celebrate one of your accomplishments increases your contentment because personal celebrations add a tangible, concrete bonus to a reached goal. Next time something big happens, express thanks to God and then go celebrate with someone you love.

Rule 7: Talk to Yourself

It sounds strange, but the person you spend the most time with is yourself. You are constantly thinking about something, and there is often a direct connection between what you think and how you feel. Consider what you consider. Think about what you think about. What are you thinking about when you are not deliberately thinking? Lies enter your mind because of the evil one and our finiteness. We need to catch negative thoughts and replace them with truth:

Negative thought: Bad things always happen to me.

Redeemed thought: God works all things out for my good and his glory, even trials (Rom. 8:28).

Negative thought: I'm single because nobody wants me.

Redeemed thought: I'm beloved by God who controls my life. My union with Christ is where I find my true identity and satisfaction. I will express my desire to the Lord and trust him with the outcome.

The difference between Christian contentment and personal misery is the difference between talking to yourself and listening to yourself. Talking to yourself is an exercise that might feel unnatural at first, but over time, as you make it a habit, it will prove itself fruitful. Here's a long quote from D. Martyn Lloyd-Jones that explains what I mean:

> The main trouble in this whole matter of spiritual depression in a sense is this, that we allow our self to talk to us instead of talking to our self. Am I just trying to be deliberately paradoxical? Far from it. This is the very essence of wisdom in this matter. Have you realized that most of your unhappiness in life is due to the fact that you are listening to yourself instead of talking to yourself? Take those thoughts that come to you the moment you wake up in the morning. You have not originated them, but they start talking to you, they bring back the problem of yesterday, etc. Somebody is talking. Who is talking to you? Your self is talking to you. Now this man's treatment [in Psalm 42] was this; instead of allowing this self to talk to him, he starts talking to himself, "Why art thou cast down, O my soul?" he asks. His soul had been repressing him, crushing him. So he stands up and says: "Self, listen for a moment,

I will speak to you". Do you know what I mean? If you do not, you have but little experience.

The main art in the matter of spiritual living is to know how to handle yourself. You have to take yourself in hand, you have to address yourself, preach to yourself, question yourself. You must say to your soul: "Why art thou cast down"—what business have you to be disquieted? You must turn on yourself, upbraid yourself, condemn yourself, exhort yourself, and say to yourself: "Hope thou in God"—instead of muttering in this depressed, unhappy way. And then you must go on to remind yourself of God, Who God is, and what God is and what God has done, and what God has pledged Himself to do. Then having done that, end on this great note: defy yourself, and defy other people, and defy the devil and the whole world, and say with this man: "I shall yet praise Him for the help of His countenance, who is also the health of my countenance and my God".[15]

Rule #8: Consider Death and Eternity

Live your life in light of eternity. Life only makes sense backwards—when you reflect on your life from heaven's vantage point. Only then will you understand why God never prospered you in ways you'd wished. Only then will you understand why some of your dreams never came true. In this life, your heart is sometimes filled with anguish, lament and grief. You wonder, "I don't understand why God is allowing this to happen." But once promoted to glory, then and only then will you be able to say, "Ah, I see now!"

What you believe happens to you after you die affects the way you live now. Eternity reminds us what really matters in life. Suddenly, life seems short, and we aren't as obsessed with status, money or success. Living a life of faithful generosity to God becomes more important than self-indulgence. We're more calm, cool, collected, content.

Our discontentment points us to heaven. Some of the best joys of life are marriage, friendship and children. And yet, even if you have the best marriage and friends and children, there will be times

---

15. D. Martyn Lloyd-Jones, *Spiritual Depression: Its Causes and Cure* (Grand Rapids: Eerdmans, 1965), 20-21; emphasis added.

of disappointment. Our souls ache because we desire heavenly bliss. And that day is coming. But it's not here yet. Not being in heaven now doesn't mean you can't derive joy from it. You can, through reflecting and contemplating the reality of eternity. Reflecting on eternity provides hope as you navigate the inevitable frustrations of earthly life.

The Power of Incremental Change

Blaise Pascal was a French writer who was converted to Christ in his early thirties. He once said, "All men seek happiness. This is without exception." Why am I interested in the subject of contentment? Why are you willing to read a book on contentment? It's because we desire happiness. Some Christians think the calling of a Christian is to be utterly miserable on earth and then finally experience happiness in heaven. Heaven is our reward for lifelong misery, we think. But this notion is false. Although we cannot expect to feel perfectly fulfilled in every season of life, the Christian faith offers real, stable and noticeable happiness. It just doesn't work the way secular culture has trained you to think. If you want a sweet sense of peace and joy amidst the unexpected and turbulent waters of life, then pursue Christian contentment.

To be content is a lifelong choice that requires deliberate lifelong practice. Don't underestimate the cumulative power of little tweaks made on a consistent basis. Those little tweaks don't seem like much, but over time you will experience the best possible state of well-being for your soul.

Discussion Questions

I encourage you to read this book with others. After asking a basic question such as, "What stood out to you most in this chapter?" you can consider the questions below.

Chapter 1: What is Contentment?
1. Reread the three definitions of contentment on page three. In your own words, how would you define contentment?
2. What are some causes that lead to discontentment in society? In what areas of your life do you struggle with discontentment?
3. What are the four examples of "Counterfeit Contentment?" (p. 15) Are there any others that you'd add to the list?
4. What are some common ways that contentment has been misapplied or misunderstood?
5. Why is contentment so important to cultivate in your own personal life?

Chapter 2: Signs and Symptoms
1. David says, "The root of all sin is the sin of discontentment" (p. 27). Do you agree? Why or why not?
2. Consider the five opponents of contentment (p. 28). Are there any others you'd add to the list?
3. Of the five opponents of contentment, which one do you struggle with the most and why?
4. When was the last time you grumbled? If grumbling is such a serious sin, why do so many people overlook it as being a minor issue?

Chapter 3: The Secret

1. What is the secret to contentment?
2. How is Philippians 4:13 often misapplied? What's the correct interpretation of this verse?
3. What does it mean to rejoice in the Lord?
4. Do you agree that it's harder to be content in seasons of prosperity than in seasons of suffering? Why or why not?

Chapter 4: Money and Possessions

1. Why do Christians have a complicated relationship with money and possessions?
2. How can you enjoy your money and possessions without turning them into idols?
3. What are the sins in our hearts that hold us back from leveraging our money and possessions for the kingdom of God?
4. How can we grow in generosity?

Chapter 5: Pain and Suffering

1. What is a thorn in your flesh? Do you currently have any?
2. How can you be content when life is hard?
3. How do you lament?
4. How was Paul able to endure in his ministry despite much pain and suffering?

Chapter 6: Success and Work

1. What is success?
2. What does the story of Billy Graham teach us about the nature of success in a fallen world?
3. How does the way a Christian views success differ from the way an unbeliever views it?
4. How much control do you have over your success? How does this provide contentment?

5. Is ambition bad? Why or why not?
6. How do you find your calling?
7. How can you pursue success while remaining faithful to God?

Chapter 7: Big God Thoughts

1. What is theology? How does theology relate to contentment?
2. What does it mean to live in a fallen world? Why are we often so surprised by suffering and hardship while living in the twenty-first century?
3. What do your sins deserve in light of God's holiness? How should this affect the way we live?
4. How does God's providence provide comfort and joy in life?

Chapter 8: Eight Rules for Contentment

1. Reread Edward Pusey's five rules for contentment. Which one resonates with you the most and why?
2. Why is it so important to God that we express thankfulness to him? How can you grow in becoming more thankful?
3. Of the eight rules mentioned for contentment, which one do you need to work on the most?
4. Are there any other rules that you would add to this list?
5. What's one practical action that you will take this week to help you experience contentment?
6. How do you want your life to look differently as a result of reading this book?

Acknowledgments

In his popular book, *The 7 Habits of Highly Effective People*, author Stephen Covey lists habits that require both independence and interdependence. First, you need to personally develop habits of independence, and then you need to recognize your need for others; success is indisputably interdependent. Both are required, according to Covey, for a successful life. Such is also true as a writer. An author must have talent and grit and read voraciously (independence). But he also must be dependent on publishers, editors, his community, family and friends (interdependence). As such, the acknowledgments section of a book reveals the interdependent aspect of an author's book.

Of course, first and foremost, I give thanks to the Triune God. Thank you for the gift of salvation, for making yourself known, for your glorious character that compels me to write.

I'm thankful for my incredible wife, Denise, for whom this book is dedicated. I love you. And I love our precious kids so much. Thank you for your love and support both in marriage and in ministry.

Thank you to Christian Focus Publications for taking a risk on a first-time author. I was overflowing with gratitude when I discovered my dream of being an author would come true. A few days prior to discovering I landed a book contract with Christian Focus, I just so happened to be in Proverbs for my devotional Bible reading, and read: "Like cold water to a thirsty soul, so is good news from a far country" (Prov. 25:25). And two days later, I got good news from Scotland.

Thank you to Colin Fast for all the help you provided. Thank you to Darrel Girardier for the blogging mentorship over the years. Your advice has helped me to go further in blogging than I would have gone had I tried building my site strictly on my own.

I'm thankful to Tim Lusk. I appreciate the permission and time to pursue this book for the broader church. Thank you for your mentorship. I genuinely enjoy your company. Thank you for believing in me.

I'm also thankful for the pastoral mentorship of Bill Kynes. Whether it's eating at In-N-Out Burger in Hollywood, looking for a car to rent late at night, or talking theology and ministry in your study, I'm thankful to call you a confidant.

One of the best decisions I made in this book writing process was to give the manuscript to five trusted friends for feedback. It was humbling to receive the feedback, but it no doubt made the book stronger. So thank you to Chris Mullally, and the mother–daughter duo, Shannon and Arden Jacquot. I also appreciate helpful feedback related to content, theology and application from Mark Ryan and Noah Wiersema.

I'm thankful for Eastside Community Church in Jacksonville, Florida for being such a receptive, warm and loving congregation to serve.

Kevin Halloran was willing to give counsel and support during my book publishing process. Reagan Rose opened a door for me. Thank you both.

I tried to share personal stories with with accuracy. But working from memory and relying on the input of others may mean a detail was occasionally off. But this, of course, doesn't change the main point of the story. A family name change led me to edit a few of the illustrations when referring to myself.

I'm grateful for Covenant Theological Seminary, where I earned a Master of Divinity degree. Any display of depth and breadth as a preacher or writer is partly due to my time at Covenant. My time at Covenant shaped me in more ways than I probably realize.

Also by Christian Focus Publications:

THE
ENVY
OF Eve

FINDING CONTENTMENT IN
A COVETOUS WORLD

MELISSA B. KRUGER

ISBN: 978-1-84550-775-6

The Envy of Eve
Finding Contentment in a Covetous World
Melissa B. Kruger

What's truly at the heart of our desires?
The Envy of Eve guides readers to understand how desires grow
into covetousness and what happens when this sin takes power
in our hearts. Covetousness chokes out the fruit of the Spirit
in our lives, allowing discontentment to bloom. The key to
overcoming is to get to the root of our problem: unbelief–a
mistrust of God's sovereignty and goodness. An ideal resource
for deeper study or group discussion.

Melissa B. Kruger
Melissa B. Kruger serves as director of Women's Initiatives for
The Gospel Coalition. Her husband, Michael J. Kruger, is the
president of Reformed Theological Seminary in Charlotte. She
wrote *The Envy of Eve* and is a speaker at various Christian
conferences across the United States.

God's Way
of Peace

Overcoming Anxiety
by Walking with God

Horatius
Bonar

Foreword by Matt Boswell

ISBN: 978-1-5271-0609-3

God's Way of Peace
Overcoming Anxiety by Walking with God
Horatius Bonar

- Peace found only in Christ
- Reason for peace found in Christ's completed work
- New edition of classic work

This book for those who are anxious gently directs our eyes back to Jesus. Taking the whole message of the gospel, Horatius Bonar shows us that although we cannot save ourselves by our character or our works, we can have peace in the finished work of Jesus Christ.

Horatius Bonar
Horatius Bonar (1808–1889) was a minister in Scotland for over fifty years. He is best known today as the writer of many great hymns.

Olan Stubbs

WHAT
to do with
WORRY

*Why Playing God
Never Works*

ISBN: 978-1-5271-0898-1

What to do with Worry
Why Playing God Never Works
Olan Stubbs

- Viewing worry as a sin
- Trusting God to deal with worry
- Victory over sin in Christ

One of the clearest and repeated things the Bible tells us about worry is: Don't. This short book is designed to help us understand worry all the way down to its roots and all the way up to its worst fruits. By the blood of Christ, we can see progressive and sustainable victory over worry in our lives. Olan Stubb's wise book is an ideal read for anyone who struggles with worry.

Olan Stubbs
Olan Stubbs is Director of Campus Outreach at Briarwood Presbyterian Church in Birmingham, Alabama. He is a husband and father of four.

EDWARD T.
WELCH

SERIES EDITED BY
JOHN PERRITT

A STUDENT'S GUIDE TO
ANXIETY

ISBN: 978-1-5271-0450-1

Track: Anxiety
A Student's Guide to Anxiety
Edward T. Welch

- How to deal with anxiety
- For younger adults
- Part of the 'Track' series

We all know the feeling. That nervous, jittery, tense feeling that tells you that something bad is just ahead. Anxiety can be overwhelming. But the Bible has plenty to say to people who are anxious. This book will help us to take our eyes off our circumstances and fix them on God.

Edward T. Welch
Counselor & Faculty at Christian Counseling and Educational Foundation and author of 'When People Are Big and God is Small', 'Running Scared', and 'Shame Interrupted'

Christian Focus Publications

Our mission statement –

STAYING FAITHFUL

In dependence upon God we seek to impact the world through literature faithful to His infallible Word, the Bible. Our aim is to ensure that the Lord Jesus Christ is presented as the only hope to obtain forgiveness of sin, live a useful life and look forward to heaven with Him.

Our books are published in four imprints:

CHRISTIAN FOCUS

Popular works including biographies, commentaries, basic doctrine and Christian living.

CHRISTIAN HERITAGE

Books representing some of the best material from the rich heritage of the church.

MENTOR

Books written at a level suitable for Bible College and seminary students, pastors, and other serious readers. The imprint includes commentaries, doctrinal studies, examination of current issues and church history.

CF4•K

Children's books for quality Bible teaching and for all age groups: Sunday school curriculum, puzzle and activity books; personal and family devotional titles, biographies and inspirational stories – because you are never too young to know Jesus!

Christian Focus Publications Ltd,
Geanies House, Fearn, Ross-shire,
IV20 1TW, Scotland, United Kingdom.
www.christianfocus.com